MARCO

COS TA RICA

U.S.A

Gulf of Mexico

THE BAHAMAS

CUBA

DOM. REP.

Mexico City

JAMAICA   HAITI

MEXICO   BELIZE
HONDURAS
GUATEMALA

Caribbean Sea

EL SALVADOR   NICARAGUA   VENEZUELA

San José

COSTA
RICA   PANAMA

Cocos Island
(C. R.)   COLOMBIA

www.marco-polo.com

THE TOURING APP

shows you the way...
including routes and offline maps!

FREE!

GET MORE OUT OF YOUR MARCO POLO GUIDE

IT'S AS SIMPLE AS THIS

1 go.marco-polo.com/cri

2 download and discover

GO!

WORKS OFFLINE!

SYMBOLS

INSIDER TIP	Insider Tip
★	Highlight
●●●●	Best of …
☼	Scenic view
♺	Responsible travel: fair trade principles and the environment respected
(*)	Telephone numbers that are not toll-free

PRICE CATEGORIES HOTELS

Expensive	over 96,000 colones
Moderate	48,000–96,000 colones
Budget	under 48,000 colones

Average prices for a double room only. Expect prices to be higher at peak season (Oct–March) and lower at low season

PRICE CATEGORIES RESTAURANTS

Expensive	over 12,300 colones
Moderate	6,200–12,300 colones
Budget	under 6,200 colones

Prices are for a typical plated dish at that establishment without drinks

On the cover: Depositing eggs on turtle beach p. 85 | Aerial tram to the jungle p. 71

CONTENTS

DID YOU KNOW?
Timeline → p. 14
Local specialities → p. 28
Costa-Rican rodeo → p. 57
Iguanas → p. 59
Beef to burgers → p. 68
Saving turtles → p. 84
Public holidays → p. 107
Budgeting → p. 111
Haven for escapists → p. 112
Currency converter → p. 113
Weather → p. 115

MAPS IN THE GUIDEBOOK
(118 A1) Page numbers and coordinates refer to the road atlas
(U A1) refers to the map of San José inside the back cover
(0) Site/address located off the map
Coordinates are also given for places that are not marked on the road atlas

(🗺 A–B 2–3) refers to the removable pull-out map
(🗺 a–b 2–3) refers to the additional inset map on the pull-out map

INSIDE FRONT COVER:
The best Highlights

INSIDE BACK COVER:
Pull-out map

The best MARCO POLO Insider Tips

Our top 15 Insider Tips

INSIDER TIP **Welcome on the river**
Casa Turire is a plantation house that combines nature, sport and culture. It's the perfect starting point for a visit to the Guayabo archaeological site → **p. 40**

INSIDER TIP **Sun salutation on a farm**
The finca *La Flor de Paraíso* near Paraíso not only farms organically, but furthermore offers visitors (including day visitors) excellent yoga lessons → **p. 38**

INSIDER TIP **Strolling through the treetops**
You'll need a good head for heights: the *Puentes Colgantes* near La Fortuna are spectacular suspension bridges in the jungle (photo above) → **p. 54**

INSIDER TIP **Go back a hundred years**
The *Museo de Cultura Popular*, situated a few kilometres north-east of Heredia, offers an insight into life in the 19th century – with meals → **p. 42**

INSIDER TIP **Caring for monkey and wildcats**
Injured, orphaned and confiscated wild animals are cared for at the *Centro de Rescate Jaguar* on the Caribbean coast (photo on right) → **p. 84**

INSIDER TIP **Relaxing in volcanic water**
Heavenly: relaxing in the hot water of the *Termales Los Laureles* – with views of Arenal Volcano → **p. 54**

INSIDER TIP **Enlightenment not ruled out**
Meditation, yoga and good food: the spiritual community *Pacha Mama* on Nicoya Peninsula invites guests to spend a couple of weeks meditating with kindred spirits → **p. 63**

INSIDER TIP **Try your hand at ornithology**
An organisation for tropical studies in Palo Verde offers rustic accommodation, vegetarian meals and fabulous opportunities for observing animals → **p. 63**

INSIDER TIP **On a jetty beside the canal**
At the *Budda Café*, situated beside the canal in the middle of Tortuguero, you sit beside the water on a wooden jetty and enjoy the surroundings, the food – and yourself → **p. 85**

INSIDER TIP **All the tacos you can eat**
Small but fabulous: the *Taquería Taco Taco* in Santa Elena is basically a taco stand, although there are a few seats just next door. But you won't find tastier tacos anywhere else → **p. 59**

INSIDER TIP **To the jungle on horseback**
In Santa Elena, *Sabine's "smiling horses"* look forward to a hack – through the jungle and over the hills → **p. 60**

INSIDER TIP **Trekking in the wilderness**
An *eco organisation* offers *river tours and treks* to the Caribbean jungle, and will visit *indígenas* in the jungle with you → **p. 83**

INSIDER TIP **On water – with wind and without**
Tico Windsurf on Lake Arenal not only offers excellent surfing, but you can also glide across the water with a kite. And if there's absolutely no wind at all, why not try stand-up paddling → **p. 53**

INSIDER TIP **Like being with old friends**
The 70-year-old *Bar La Bomba* in Golfito has been skilfully refurnished and brightened up with some antique finds. The beer is really excellent, and you can listen to the manifold stories of the *ticos* and newcomers → **p. 67**

INSIDER TIP **To the hotel by minibus**
It's possible to travel around Costa Rica in comfort even without a hire car or taxi. The private bus company *Quality Transfers* transports travellers from one accommodation to the next inexpensively and reliably → **p. 114**

BEST OF ...

FOR FREE

● *Visit a national hero*
In Alejuela in a historic building opposite the central park, work on a *Museum for Juan Santamaría* is underway. The *ticos* love the building because cultural events are often held here – and admission is free → p. 33

● *Palm beaches and a coral reef*
The *Cahuita National Park* on the Caribbean coast is famous, amongst other things, for its marine flora and fauna. There are two entrances: access is free (donations gratefully accepted) via Kelly Creek, which is close to the wonderful sandy beaches (photo) → p. 82

● *Museum in the High School*
The neoclassical high school of Cartago is home to the *Museo Histórico-Etnográfico* with weapons and armoury from the colonial times and finds from the pre-Columbian period. One of the halls is laid out like a colonial house → p. 37

● *Open-air films by the water*
Casablanca, Forrest Gump, Out of Africa: classics and blockbusters are shown on the free *Outdoor Movie Nights* in Quepos between January and March. Make yourself comfortable in the open-air theatre in the harbour, get yourself a beer – and enjoy! → p. 71

● *Living wooden figures in the "House of the Dreamer" in the Orosí valley*
The outside of this house, which is made from old wood, is decorated with lifelike carved wooden figures. On the inside are shelves with numerous works produced by a wood carver and sculptor: a universe of unbelievable characters and the country's revered saints → p. 41

● *To the MADC on Mondays*
Favourite spot in San José for students and art-lovers: on Mondays, artists display their pictures and installations at the *Museum of Contemporary Art and Design,* a former liqueur distillery with all the morbid charm of an old factory building → p. 41

○○○● Dots in guidebook refer to "Best of..." tips

● *Butterfly garden*

The *Butterfly Conservatory* is beside Lake Arenal: a creature that is a beautiful as a flower and flies like a bird – you'll really appreciate the miracle of it here. Not only is it home to most butterfly varieties, but it also protects and breeds the insects and other rainforest creatures (photo) → p. 54

● *Hike around a volcano crater*

Not only can you climb the *Volcán Poás*, but you can also walk around its crater. This is followed by a path through dense vegetation to a second crater with a lake – dress warmly! → p. 35

● *Zip over waterfalls*

Glide effortlessly through the jungle on zip lines, as the steel cables are called. The *Adventure Park* of the Finca Daniel has two dozen different zip lines over eleven waterfalls and other sights; quite an adventure – even for the less athletic → p. 100

● *On the trail of the blue-jeans frog*

Bright blue legs, a red body – the *blue-jeans dart frog* is the most striking and prettiest of the many types of frog found in Costa Rica. This little fellow is found in most of the national parks, and also at the *Frog Garden* of the *Rainforest Aerial Tramway* or at the *Inbioparque* – and spotting one is said to bring you luck! → p. 44

● *Ecology and luxury combined*

Until a few years ago, Costa Rica's eco lodges tended to be rather rustic affairs, but today comfort and style rule. The best example is the *El Silencio Lodge & Spa* near Sarchí, which is green and environmentally friendly, and where the rooms are so lovely that you won't want to leave → p. 36

● *Children's rainforest*

What once started out as a small nature reserve, the *Bosque Eterno de Los Niños* in Monteverde has received such excellent support that it now covers an area of more than 77 mi². Huge tree ferns, giant moss-covered trees, forests of orchids with the colourful Quetzal flying over them. A visit to the land of the natural parks is a unique and yet typical experience → p. 57

ONLY IN

BEST OF ...

● *Coffee tour around the volcano*
The traditional coffee company *Doka Estate* on the slopes of the Poás Volcano introduces you to the world of roasting and grinding. The buffets at the restaurant La Cajuela are delicious, and there are colourful painted metal mugs and coffee in the shop (photo) → p. 34

● *Aquarium in the old railway station*
The site of the old railway station of Puntarena has been turned into the *Parque Marino del Pacífico* – with aquariums, turtle and crocodile terrariums, pelican aviaries and a petting pool → p. 73

● *Café au lait at the National Theatre*
The capital's *Café* in the Teatro Nacional radiates the atmosphere of the years of origin. Wall murals, black-and-white photos, Art Nouveau lamps and marble: it's the perfect place to spend an afternoon → p. 47

● *Through the rainforest in wellies*
Waterproof footwear and a rain jacket – that's all that is required to enjoy the *Parque Nacional Manuel Antonio* even in the rain. It stays warm during the rainy season, when there are not so many visitors and a dense leaf canopy offers protection against the rain → p. 75

● *Indoor rainforest*
The *Inbioparque* in Heredia has everything: dry and cloud forests with all their animals, tropical plants, orchids and heliconia. If it rains, pop inside to experience the forest in the halls → p. 44

● *Solid gold!*
The National Bank of Costa Rica in San José not only has gold bars, but is also home to the *Museo del Oro Precolombino:* figurines, jewellery from earrings to bracelets and necklaces, figures of deities and animals from a dozen centuries → p. 46

RAIN

RELAX AND CHILL OUT
Take it easy and spoil yourself

● *Sundowner with views*
At the restaurant *Anfiteatro* in Jacó, the food comes second after the fabulous views. You look down onto massive trees covered in orchids and epiphytes. And at night, the starry sky over the Pacific is a tremendous sight → **p. 70**

● *Hot volcanic water*
The *Eco Termales La Fortuna* offers five pools at different temperatures. The spring water is heated by the active volcano, Arenal. It takes a maximum of 100 people, an arrangement that guarantees peace and relaxation → **p. 54**

● *Relaxation by the tropical forest*
The little hotel *Villa Romantica* is on the outskirts of Quepos on the road to Manuel Antonio: heavenly peace, interrupted only by the amusing monkeys and birds. Whether in the restaurant or by the romantic pool, you'll find yourself here → **p. 77**

● *Floating among the treetops*
Enjoy a gondola ride through the rainforest. Experience pure nature on the *Rainforest Aerial Tramway* and find yourself almost at the point of meditative relaxation → **p. 44**

● *Hotel spa at La Fortuna*
The resort hotel *The Springs* has no fewer than 18 thermal pools. The temperatures ranging from 24 °C to 32 °C/75 °F to 90 °F will banish every trace of stress from your body and mind. And if that's not enough relaxation for you, then continue the process at one of the country's best spas (photo) → **p. 54**

● *Green boutique hotel*
There's probably no nicer way to start the day than with breakfast at the hotel *Gaia* in Quepos: the views of the dense green leafy canopy and the blue of the ocean, starched linen napkins and the smiling 5-star service – and every dish is absolutely delicious → **p. 76**

INTRODUCTION

DISCOVER COSTA RICA!

Bubbling volcanoes that light up the night sky with a firework display of glowing red magma, *butterflies the size of your palm* and *tiny hummingbirds* that draw the nectar from the jungle flowers, Swiss entrepreneurs who became eco hoteliers and Germans who run a flying school for microlights. *Trekking through the cloud forest* and canoe trips through Caribbean lagoons, a sundowner on a lookout terrace high above the Pacific, and a *visit to an organic coffee plantation*. Travel by 4-wheel drive to lodges in the rainforest and relax on dark sandy beaches – some experiences you can only have in Costa Rica, and they will leave any all-inclusive luxury holiday in the shade.

Costa Rica, the *country with no war and no cold weather*, one of America's oldest democracies, has little in common with its neighbours apart from its geographic location: positioned between crisis-ridden Nicaragua and Panama known for its canal, in the middle of the land bridge between North and South America. American national parks are famous all over the world, but it's usually the ones in the USA that spring to mind when we hear reports of fabulous natural beauties. And yet just a few hours' flight from the US national parks Yosemite and Grand Canyon lies Costa Rica where,

Have you ever seen a lovelier beach? Playa Espadilla in the Manuel Antonio National Park

since the early 1970s, *more than 30 regions have been designated as protected areas*. Probably unique in the world: over one-quarter of this country is protected – as national parks and biosphere reserves, but also with Indian reservations and areas that are UNESCO World Heritage Sites. Steaming rainforests, *mist-shrouded high valleys*, ochre savannahs, mangrove swamps and dry forests, mountain chains and volcanoes, meandering rivers, *coral reefs* and green islands off the coast: they are all part of the country's unusual beauty, and worthy of protection.

Small wonder that Costa Rica has become the synonym for eco-friendly activity holidays, a place of pilgrimage for ecologists and biologists. In fact, in many respects the country embodies the *ideal of the tropical paradise*. Yet the situation once looked pretty dire – two-thirds of the rainforest had already fallen

From 500 BC
Three tribes develop in what is now Costa Rica under the influence of migrants from South and North America: Huetares both in the Valle Central and on the Caribbean coast, Chorotega in the north of Costa Rica and southern Nicaragua, and Boruca on the southern Pacific and in the north of Panama

800–1400 AD
The heyday of Guayabo, a Huetares settlement close to what is now Cartago, with roads, bridges, aqueducts and stone dwellings

1502
Christopher Columbus lands on the island of Uvita off Puerto Limón, and

victim to mankind's greed for money before people realised the danger, and listed various areas as protected zones and issued more stringent conservation laws. However, this was also for other reasons: the country's income from coffee and banana exports was not enough to cover its foreign debt and balance the state budget. Which made it even more important that the country preserve its most important resource and *make the rainforest economically viable without destroying it* – a difficult task that Costa Rica wants to resolve by marketing the forest to tourists.

On the search for El Dorado, the legendary hoard of gold, Christopher Columbus reached the country's Atlantic coast in 1502 and name it Costa Rica, the "Rich Coast". But instead of the gold they had hoped for, the Spaniards encountered lush vegetation – the very thing that

today, as the Costa Ricans have recognised, is indeed worth gold. The *tourist flow* that started coming here a number of years ago is indeed bringing the country much-needed currency, and today accounts for about one-tenth of its employment. Costa Rica has learnt from

> **Christopher Columbus discovered the "Rich Coast" in 1502**

the mistakes made by other countries: *class instead of mass* is the motto, and it opts for quality rather than giant hotels and cheap tourism. And although this level of tourism might cost the visitors a few colones more, it is more than worth it for the country and its nature. National parks are closed from time to time if concerns arise that the volume of visitors is threatening to damage the nature.

calls the land Costa Rica ("Rich Country")

1563
The Spanish establish Cartago and make it the capital, which it remains until 1823

1821
Independence from Spain, Costa Rica becomes part of the Mexican empire

1848
Proclaimed a republic

1899
The United Fruit Company of the USA takes over the banana trade

1948
José María Figueres Ferrer becomes president and

15

Eco tourism is the order of the day. This includes lower hotel buildings that blend with the landscape and are made from natural materials, and choosing local products over imports. As yet, the only hotel high-rises are in San José, but there are more *lodges, cabinas* and *cabañas,* wooden buildings in the middle of the countryside, *that run on solar power and have their own fresh water supply*. Guests follow specially-made *senderos,* hiking trails, that meander through the natural parks for an initial impression of the sheer variety of the tropical flora and fauna. For further clarification, consider the – otherwise – boring statistics: 900 tree species; 1,200 orchids; 230 mammal species including *jaguars, pumas, coatis, monkeys, sloths*, anteaters and raccoons; 860 bird species including 50 different hummingbirds and 15 parrots; and 40,000 types of insect including *3,000 different types of butterfly*. This area, which covers around 0.01 percent of the total surface of the earth – roughly the size of Switzerland – is home to five percent of all the flora and fauna on the planet.

> **The synonym for eco-friendly active holidays**

The Cordillera Volcánica runs through the country parallel to the Pacific. This is a volcanic mountain range with 70 volcanoes (five of them are still active), the peaks of which measure *over 3,000 m/9,843 ft* and form a meteorological divide: hot and humid with frequent rain on the Caribbean side, in a six-monthly cycle with the dry and rainy season on the Pacific coast. People have settled on the fertile high plains of the Cordillera since the turn of time, and this is also where the Spanish settled after they took possession of Costa Rica in the 16th century.

> **Of its 70 volcanoes, five are still active**

It was a further 200 years after the Spanish conquest that they created what is today the city centre of San José, Spanish and straight-lined, and dedicated to St Joseph. Its magnificent buildings are today often sought in vain. Repeated earthquakes have destroyed many of the Spanish churches, baroque palaces and homes, and only ruins remain.

starts a system of social welfare; a year later the army is disbanded

1987 President Óscar Arias Sánchez receives the Nobel Peace Prize for his service in the Nicaragua conflict

2016 Turrialba Volcano erupts in May. The ash cloud measuring 3,000 m/9,843 ft in height covers several towns and cities, and reaches San José 40 km/24.9 mi away

2018 Carlos Alvarado Quesada, born in 1980, is elected President by the left-leaning PAC

Ticos is the Costa Ricans slightly tongue-in-cheek name for themselves

"Our temples and palaces are our nature," as the Costa Ricans say: There are only a few structural sights dating back to the pre-Columbian population left. Before Columbus's arrival, three *Indian tribes* lived in what is now Costa Rica, in the shadow of the Mayans who had settled to the north. Instead of palaces, temples and monumental architecture, they left only a few small settlements behind – but they also left ceramics, stone artefacts, figures and jewellery. The mysterious stone spheres of the Boruca are an assortment of over three hundred petrospheres.

The Caribbean love of life is documented by the wooden houses on the Caribbean coast painted in the bright "candy" colours turquoise, yellow and pink. Some are on stilts, and almost all of them have an all-round veranda. Visitors enjoy the climate and sea, beach and jungle, and the Caribbean zest for life and lightness. Many of them came from abroad to live in Costa Rica: *American Quakers*, who cleared the forests to develop dairy farming and agriculture; *pensioners*, who wanted to enjoy a better standard of living than at home, and even *environmentally-aware settlers*, who wanted to live and work in harmony with nature.

The country's unsolved problems include the high population growth, which is causing additional pressure on the residential areas, and creating a need for new jobs. As yet, this tiny country embodies an *exemplary model of eco-friendly living*. *Pura vida*, as they say in Costa Rica. "Discover Costa Rica!" is nothing more than: discover pure life!

WHAT'S HOT

1 From nature

Wellness Volcanic sand and rainforest mud leave the skin as soft and smooth as a baby's – the spa of the *Four Seasons (Península Papagayo) (photo)* in Guanacaste is all about natural beauty products. Lavender, cucumber and aloe vera are used as a mask on a sun-stressed body at the *Harmony Hotel (Nosara)*. It provides the skin with plenty of moisture. Ylang-ylang and milk are the main ingredients in the wellness bath at the *Pacífica Spa* of the *Hotel Parador (Manuel Antonio)*.

Well rolled

2

Sushi Of course, fish and rice are used for Costa Rican sushi, but local specialities are also essential. At the *Sensu (Plaza Los Laureles | Escazú)*, for instance, where turrialba cheese is one of the ingredients that is used in the rolls. The Japanese chef at *Tropical Sushi* in Quepos also rolls fusion makis and nigiris. Authentic (and inexpensive) sushi is served at the *Okami Sushi Restaurante (www.okamisushi.net)* in San José; all sorts of delicacies made from fish and rice are served in the small restaurant from 11.30am.

Sulphur & sea spray

3

Action Costa Rica is the perfect place for lovers of adventure. Rafting on the rushing rivers is the country's latest trend. The professionals at *Rancho Los Tucanes (Manuel Antonio | Puntarenas)* hurl themselves into the rapids of the Río Naranjo with their clients. Things heat up on an excursion with *Adventure Manuel Antonio (Manuel Antonio | Puntarenas)*. They take you up the Arenal – this volcano is considered one of the most active in the world. Abseiling and canyoning with *Costa Rica Ríos (www.costaricarios.com)* take you in the opposite direction with canoe rides on rivers with different levels of difficulty.

Pot gazers

Cookery courses Some find the local cuisine a little repetitive. However, that this is not so is confirmed by the cookery courses offered by Sibyl at the *Casas Pelícano (Playa Junquillal | www. casas-pelicano.com) (photo)*. Aromatic fish is wrapped up in banana leaves or a delicious soup prepared from pumpkin, oranges and shrimps – a new experience for Costa Rican participants. On the eastern coast, Miss Edith shares secrets from her kitchen. The restaurant named after her and famed for its Caribbean cuisine is known all over Cahuita. The mountainous heartland is where you will find the *Casa Mettá (San José de la Montaña)* that provides insights into Costa Rican cuisine. Vegan dishes are one of chef Wendy's specialities. There are even more offers to be found at *www.costaricacooking.com*.

Under a leafy canopy

Sleeping Tree houses are "in" all over the world, but building with wood in the midst of nature is perfect for the tropics – at the *Tree Houses Hotel (Santa Clara | San Carlos | treehouseshotelcostarica.com) (photo)* you'll sleep surrounded by the green of the trees. The dense rainforest with sea views is also home to the *Lapa Rios Rain Forest Wilderness Lodge (Lapa Rios, Playa Carbonera | Puerto Jiménez | Península de Osa | www. laparios.com)*. It's also not far to the sand at the *Tree House Lodge (Punta Uva | Limón | www.costaricatreehouse.com)* at Puerto Viejo Beach. To be at one with nature, head for the *Laguna del Lagarto Lodge (Boca Tapada | www.lagarto-lodge-costa-rica.com)* at the heart of 1.9 mi² of rainforest. The numerous hiking paths through the unspoilt nature are wonderful.

IN A NUTSHELL

GREEN AND BLUE

Green and blue are the colours of the landscape: the green of the banana trees, the blue of the plastic bags filled with ripening fruits and soaked in insecticide. Bananas are today a major economic factor in Costa Rica, and the country is the world's second biggest exporter of the fruit. Cultivation and marketing began at the end of the 19th century. Along with coffee, banana became the island's main export, enabling it to become independent of American groups and financial backers.

WHO LIVES HERE?

Eighty percent of the 4.9 million *ticos* are white – as descendants of the Spanish, this gives them a special position among the inhabitants of Latin America. Only 15 percent of the population are Mestizos (to compare: in Mexico the figure is 80 percent), that is, descendants of whites and indigenous peoples. One percent of the population is black, 1 percent Chinese, and 1.5 percent *indígenas*; the descendants of the original Indian inhabitants – around 55,000 of them live in 35 small reserves – are among the poorest population groups. As the right to political asylum is rooted in Costa Rica's constitution, the tiny country became a haven for many thousands of refugees from El Salvador and Nicaragua. The population growth is high, and the average number of children per family is five. Almost 90 percent of the population is Roman Catholic.

Bananas, conservation etc.: in this "banana republic" that doesn't have an army, only the animals have shells

MOONLIGHT FLIT

Some enjoy them as an appetiser or soup, others like to wear them as jewellery. Despite numerous conventions on the international trade in endangered species, turtle eggs, meat and shells are still processed and exported in the tropics. Some species of this animal, which has been on the planet for around 100 million years, face extinction. Costa Rica has decided to protect them, and a number of research stations study, identify, protect – and raise them. Thousands of turtles swim onto the island from both of the adjoining oceans, laboriously clambering onto the sand in the moonlight when the tide is in, and digging holes 50 cm/20 in deep for their eggs. Some of them weigh several hundred kg, and their nocturnal progress is therefore as slow as you would expect – although this is something that tourists are able to watch provided they observe a few safety measures, i.e. no light and no noise. The eggs spend six to eight weeks hatching in the sun (provided no one digs them up first), after which up to 100 tiny turtles scramble up through the layer of sand and instantly head out to sea. Sadly, many of them don't make it, falling victim to man, birds and fish.

all the way back to the Ice Age, but today is at risk by man and the environmental influences we have caused. Only 50 years ago, Costa Rica's rainforest (in the tropical lowland regions) and cloud forest (at heights above 1,000 m/3,281 ft) covered over 70 percent of the land.

Dainty aerial acrobats are also at home in the cloud forests of the natural parks

JUNGLE SECRETS

It is not unusual for many of the thousands of different trees in the Costa Rican rainforest to grow to heights of 40 m/131.2 ft and more. In fact, this forest – which today only covers less than ten percent of the earth's surface – is home to more than half of all the world's flora and fauna. Life in the jungle is lived on various levels – dark, hot and extremely moist on the ground. Life in the treetops is largely unresearched. The most stable but also the most sensitive eco system in the world, millions of years old, has survived climate changes

MOUNTAINS AND TROPICS

Measuring a total of 19,768 mi² (about the same size as Switzerland), Costa Rica is the third-smallest country on the American mainland. Its topography is largely defined by mountains, and is dominated by 70 volcanoes, both extinct and active. This cordillera runs across the country from the north-west to the south-east, and acts like a meteorological divide. The highest mountain is Chirripó at 3,819 m/12,530 ft. A vast lowland range follows the Atlantic coast, a wet tropical region of tropical swamps, lagoons and rivers. The capital San José and densely populated surrounded area lies in the central high plain at the foot of the Cordillera Central. The country's borders between the Atlantic coast (200 km/124 mi) and the Pacific coast (1,200 km/746 mi) are formed by Nicaragua to the north and Panama to the south.

CROSS-BORDER COMMUTERS

Many Costa Ricans believe the number of migrants from Nicaragua, which is estimated at between 500,000 and one million, is too high for the total population of around 5 million. A lot of them have entered the country illegally and are employed for the banana and coffee harvests or as housemaids, and take home between US$250 and 300 a month. Their living conditions are precarious, and they have no access to the state healthcare system, which is free for *ticos*. Furthermore, the migrants from Central America encounter emotions ranging from mistrust to open enmity, and they are held responsible for the increase in insecurity and in criminality, for attacks, break-ins and thefts. However, the children they give birth to in Costa Rica are Costa Rican nationals, and so can hope for a better future.

HEALTH INSTEAD OF WEAPONS

In 1948, a time of political unrest, the social democrat José Figueres Ferrer took on government affairs for 18 months, launched effective social reforms and a year later submitted a constitution that included the abolition of the armed forces. This measure has paid off for Costa Rica in many different ways. The money saved was instead invested in social welfare and healthcare,

in teaching the population to read and write, and in a comprehensive reform of the education system. Today, Costa Rica is unique in Latin America with these achievements – and without having suffered in any way from the lack of an army.

NATURE-LOVERS ON THE GO

🌐 Costa Rica has more than 20 national parks as well as several game and nature reserves and privately-owned forests and reservations that are maintained by hotels and guesthouses, haciendas, fincas and lodges, plus animal and nature conservation organisations. Admission charges, donations and tourist attractions (zip lines, aerial tramways etc.) are partly used for their maintenance. Access to the reservation is along specially laid paths and trails (senderos) that you can follow on your own or with a guide. As a general rule, do not try to cut costs in Costa Rica when looking for a nature guide, because without one you will see and understand far less. They are also often highly educated, full of understanding and passionate about nature and also for the interests of the Costa Rican population, and competent conversationalists. www.sinac.go.cr

ECO

🌐 Costa Rica is the world's leading destination for eco-tourism, a synonym for ecological travel that takes you close to the country's nature, ever since it identified its nature as a resource in the 1980s and developed protected areas. Today, you will be hard put to find a hotel or a provider that doesn't have the word "ecological" in its name. However, as the popularity of this tiny country grows, its delicate eco systems are starting to suffer more and more. One example is Manuel Antonio, where there are several daily flights in from San José. Every year, hundreds of thousands of visitors walk the *senderos* in the national park, which measures only 2.7 mi², with the result that the monkeys now beg for bananas and the park is closed on Mondays so staff can clear all the rubbish. In Tortuguero, tourists are transported across the canals to the lodges and crocodiles by motorboat; a slower form of transport would cause less damage. Furthermore, many of the criteria for the numerous quality seals that hotels and lodges adorn themselves with are not always transparent. Research can also provide some surprising results: large, sustainably designed hotels with ecological supply technology cause less damage to the environment than the smaller lodges that are sprouting up all over the country.

STONE GIANTS

Hundreds have been discovered so far, and it is assumed that many more are still waiting to be found: artificial stone spheres, made of granite and lava, measuring between 10 cm/4 in and 2 m/6,6 ft, perfectly rounded and weighing up to an amazing 16 tonnes. Creating the shape was not that difficult, and probably achieved by using a piece of string or rope and a sharp stone to carve a semi-circle in strong wood, which was then cut out. This produced a template, and the finishing touches were added to the stone by rotating it in the template. They can be found in the south of Costa Rica in the jungle and river estuaries, in valleys and up mountains. The spheres were probably made by the Boruca, a pre-Columbian civilization, and were possibly to symbolise astronomical alignments, as they could be used to "reproduce" them. Many were destroyed by the Spanish, who believed that there was gold inside them. Also known as the *Indian stone balls* or *spheres (www.world-mysteries.com/sar_12.htm)*, today they adorn museums, parks and public buildings. There are two in the front garden outside Paseo Colón 2044 in San José.

ON THE STREET

They await you on roads, in parks and in squares: street sellers hawking their stocks of sunglasses, watches and water, chewing gum and clothing, souvenirs and perfume. On the Plaza de la Cultura in San José they offer pigeon food, although the pigeons there have long been a pest and nuisance. If ever there is a traffic jam, whether in the city or on a country road, almost instantly goods are offered through the car windows and people start to haggle. *Ticos* and refugees from Central America, including children and teenagers, try to survive this way. As the police of San José are unable to get the situation under control, they confiscate the goods and take them away in lorries.

TICOS & TICAS

The Spanish suffixes "ito" or "ita" are a sign of friendliness. Thus *momento* becomes *momentito,* a "little moment". The Costa Ricans use "ico" as a diminutive, so they say *momentico,* and they especially like doubling this, for instance to make *hermano* (brother) *hermanitico* (tiny little brother). Because of this habit, the other Latin Americans call them *ticos,* and they are happy to be known as such.

VOLUNTEERS WANTED!

No other country offers as many opportunities for volunteers as Costa Rica, in the first instance for animal protection and conservation. The choices range from monitoring turtle eggs on the Pacific and Caribbean coasts to helping out in the nature reserves, caring for injured wild animals and teaching English to schoolchildren. At the "Flower of paradise" *La Flor de Paraíso* (see p. 38) volunteers work in organic farming, at the Botanic Gardens, in forest or stable, and are also involved in teaching about the environment. *www.la-flor.org/volunteer.html*

al cone shape, and many are disguised as "ordinary" mountains. The country owes its fertile soil to the volcanic ash. The Arenal Volcano (1,657 m/5,436 ft), 100 km/62 mi north of San José is the most active one in the country. In 1968 there was a massive eruption that left more than 80 people dead. Although its nocturnal eruptions have declined in

Stone spheres at the National Museum San José – please don't roll them away!

The organisation "Instituto Costarricense Intercultural en Español" *(http://www.icies.org/)* offers a wide range of work experience opportunities, including Spanish lessons, internships and volunteering.

VOLCANOES – QUITE HARMLESS!

There's no need to worry – volcanic eruptions are rare in Costa Rica, and usually foreseeable. The country's volcanoes also fall short of the popular image in other respects. Not all are in the tradition-

recent years, no one is allowed to climb to the top. There are several trails at the foot of the volcano such as the *West Slope Trail.*

AGRICULTURE

Natural resources are rare, and bananas, coffee, sugar, pineapple, cocoa, palm oil and beef are the country's main export products. The timber industry is also a major economic factor. Costa Rica sells high-grade woods all over the world, but balances the impact with extensive re-foresting.

FOOD & DRINK

Costa Rican cuisine isn't exactly known for its variety or sophistication, but tends to be plain and tasty. Beans – a source of protein that even makes an ideal breakfast – and maize dishes have played the main roles for centuries.

One other basic food is rice, and there are hundreds of different ways of preparing it. Rice and black beans are also the basic ingredients for the **Costa Rican national dish, casado**. The word actually means "married" – so why should this popular everyday dish be called *casado?* Well, it is said to be that which awaits a *tico* every day – and for the rest of his life – when he marries a *tica*: rice and fried black beans, and often served with scrambled eggs or sour cream. As well as fried plantain, and fried or boiled meat and salad.

Traditionally, the first meal served *in the morning* is *gallo pinto*, **the second national dish**, and again a combination of rice and black (or red) pan-fried beans, and a choice of onions, sour cream, thin maize pancakes *(tortillas),* cheese or scrambled egg. Ham, chicken or bacon can also be added to the dish.

At lunchtime and in the evening the Costa Ricans appreciate chicken or beef with their rice and beans, and eggs and fish complete the menu. The various vegetable dishes and accompaniments are excellent. Next to carrots, peppers, potatoes, pumpkin and onions, rather exotic-sounding vegetables such as **yucca and cassava roots** are also served.

The fruit pyramids on the food stalls at the markets and in the market halls are just as pleasing to the eye as to the palate

Caution is the watchword when it comes to the apparently innocuous *picadillos*, potatoes, carrots, onions and peppers preserved in chillies and diluted vinegar, which can pack a terrific punch.

Something that is new to Europeans in particular is **Creole cuisine**, where coconuts and spices play the main roles. One of the most popular stews is *rundown* (also *rondon*), which consists of meat and vegetables cooked in coconut milk. The sea is one of the country's richest treasures, and provides the Costa Ricans with fish and seafood. Mexico is the home of *ceviche*, a popular starter consisting or raw fish marinated in lemon juice and seasoned with coriander, limes and onions. Restaurants that specialise in seafood are called *marisquería*.

For **dessert** there is cheese from Monteverde (e.g. Monte Rico) or one of the many sweet dishes such as *granizado con fruta*, ice cream and fruit on crushed ice.

Costa Ricans greatly appreciate a **good beer**, and the varieties brewed in the

LOCAL SPECIALITIES

arreglado – a small sandwich made with meat, cheese or chicken

arroz con carne/pollo/pescado – rice with meat / chicken / fish

cajeta – dessert made with coconut, sugar, vanilla and milk

carne asada – fried thin slices of beef

chicharrones – crispy baked pieces of pork crackling (photo on right)

chorreado – maize pancake with sour cream

empanada – maize pancake with beans, cheese, meat and potatoes

enchilada – pastry filled with cheese, potatoes, meat

frijoles molidos – refried beans with onions and paprika

frijoles refritos – refried red or black beans

gallo – tortilla with beans, cheese, meat, tomatoes, fried potatoes

guacamole – mashed avocado with lemon juice and tomatoes (photo left)

olla de carne – stew of meat, chicken, potatoes, vegetables, maize, yucca, plantain

pan bon – dark spiced fruit bread

patacones – fried slices of plantain

patí – pasty filled with minced beef, chicken, fish or plantain

pionono – savoury plantain and black bean rolls

plátanos fritos – fried plantain

pollo asado – hot and spicy fried chicken

quesadillas – grain flour tortilla with cheese

sopa negra – black bean soup with vegetables and egg

taco – deep-fried tortilla filled with fish, meat or vegetables

tamal – cornbread filled with meat and paprika and steamed in banana or maize leaves

tostada – crispy toasted tortilla with filling

country – Bavaria, Pilsen and Imperial – can certainly stand the comparison with European beer. Wine is expensive and usually imported. Other extremely popular choices are *mixed fruit drinks (frescos),* such as puréed mango or banana topped up with milk or water, while the hotels also serve pure fruit juices. Green coconuts *(pipas),* are sold on the roadside, opened with a machete and the contents slurped through a straw – the perfect thirst-quencher, and also extremely *beneficial to those suffering from gastric problems*.

Costa Rican coffee is exported all over the world, and the locals drink it all day long. Popular **sundowners** are the delicious mixed drinks, such as *piña colada* (pineapple juice, coconut milk, rum), *daiquirí* (lemon juice, rum, crushed ice), *margarita* (lemon juice, Cointreau, Tequila), *Cuba libre* (white rum, lemon juice, cola).

There are lots of different restaurants in San José. The mid-range is dominated by **establishments geared towards US tastes**, whereas the preferred choice of the "better" native society are the **European restaurants**. In the countryside you'll find mainly **simple pubs**(sodas) serving local cuisine. Also popular are the ones that sell an extensive range of pasta and salads as well as Italian pizzas. The listed prices do not include the 15% tax and 10 to 20% service charge. If the charge for service is not added as standard, then a corresponding tip is expected.

All the bigger towns have a **central market with lots of food stalls**. You sit on wooden stools at the counter for whatever you like, from breakfast to an evening meal. With coffee and fruit and vegetable juices. And on lots of street corners you'll find a snack bar, although the offerings aren't always suitable for delicate stomachs. A *bar* can be almost anything: a pub, somewhere to eat, a café, general stall – or all of the above. The star of the Costa Rican cooking scene is **Flora Sobrado de Echandi**, known all over the country as Tía Florita. The writer of almost 20 cookbooks and the star of countless cookery shows demonstrates how the country's traditional cuisine can be varied. Her recipes (www.cocinandocontiaflorita.tv) draw on the tried-and-tested, and are updated with the use of spices and new ingredients. Unlike Mexico to the north, un-

til the recent past *ticas* hardly used hot sauces, nor did they season with chillies. In the popular tourist resorts, numerous **vegetarian restaurants** have sprung up,

Shaken, stirred and usually with rum: refreshing mixed drinks

as well as Italian, French and Asian restaurants run by foreigners – and their cooking traditions are now also influencing the regional cuisine, as is the world of fusion food from the USA, which draws on cuisines from all over the world. **Fusion food dishes** are available mainly in expensive restaurants.

SHOPPING

Bowls made from polished coconut wood, strings of shells on long tapes that are used as breezy curtains, rustic ceramics in soft earth hues: in Costa Rica, you won't have to spend a lot of money on individually made items. The art of the *artesanías,* decorative art has a long tradition in the country. The different ethnic groups in Central America were already known for their gold jewellery, ceramics and weavings in Columbus's days.

CRAFTS & TEXTILES

Fans of these styles will also find brightly embroidered, and often hand-woven, dresses, jackets, blouses and trousers on the markets. Some of these items are made in Guatemala and Mexico, or the designs are inspired by the *molas* embroidery of neighbouring Panama. What applies to the textiles also often applies to many other hand-made items: they are mostly made in different other Latin American countries and imported into Costa Rica. Visitors can only be pleased to see such a tremendous variety of skill and craft in one place.

In the town of Sarchí and the surrounding area you will find lots of artisans, and business really flourishes here with the colourful *carretas,* the traditional oxcarts that are a pretty symbol of Costa Rica. The carts are made in all possible sizes, and are also used as decorations in homes and gardens. Less striking are the many rocking chairs made of leather and wood that collapse for easy transportation.

ECO SHOPS

The ecologically orientated shops in the national parks and their surrounding areas are veritable treasure troves for lovely and practical souvenirs. You can buy hand-crafted soaps made from lime oil or mango-fragranced, exotic aromatic oils, writing paper made from banana leaves, children's T-shirts with turtle motifs, locally produced coffee and much more.

The significant number of immigrants in Costa Rica include numerous artists and artisans who create and sell their own product lines. Jewellery is particularly popular and, thanks to the tremendous abundance of tropical woods, you will easily find lavishly made wooden items such as combs, jewellery boxes, plates and bowls.

From textiles and herbal tinctures to cigars and coffee – much is now also available in organic quality

MARKETS & SHOPS

There are plenty of shopping opportunities in the capital, although prices there are higher than elsewhere in the country or if you buy directly from the producer, although the quality is usually good. And there is more choice. There are also lots of specialist shops, although people usually buy on the street, where the street vendors display their goods, and at markets. Every village has its *mercado central,* a treasure trove for anything from medicinal herbs and tinctures to shoes, rugs and hand-carved combs.

Communications centres in rural areas are the numerous *pulperías,* grocer's shops that sell spices and cigarettes, shampoo and milk powder. However, these stands and little shops, which are also known as *pulpe* and *minisúper*, are facing an increasing threat from the major supermarkets.

WHAT YOU SHOULDN'T BUY

The grey market concerns not only tortoise shell and products made from it, but also sea snails and shells that are protected by the Washington Convention, the Convention on International Trade in Endangered Species of Wild Fauna and Flora.

As with the purchase of tortoise shell, the acquisition of giant snails also has serious consequences: instead of collecting flotsam and jetsam, when demand is high the creatures are caught and killed for tourists. Please do not buy these "souvenirs" or anything else made from tortoise shell or iguana skin. And if you want to buy items made of wood, please carefully ensure that the wood is grown in plantations so you don't inadvertently promote the deforestation of the ecologically invaluable tropical rainforest.

CENTRAL PLATEAU

The country's treasure chest: Meseta Central (or Valle Central) is the central plateau in the middle of the country, between 1,000 and 1,700 m/3,280 and 5,577 ft and surrounded by three mountain ranges, mountains and extinct as well as active volcanoes.

Coffee bushes thrive on the fertile soil and have brought wealth and prosperity to the region. As well as San José, the modern capital, you will also find lots of old Spanish towns that radiate all the charm of the past, and San José has some of the best museums in the whole of Central America.

It will only take you an hour to get to the dark beaches on the Pacific Ocean. Pleasant temperatures – the annual average is 22 °C/72 °F – a reliable dry season and the excellent public transport system plus a tremendous choice of hotels and restaurants increase the appeal and attraction of this charming landscape for tourists, with volcanoes and nature reserves that are easy to get to from San José. The area is home to over half of all Costa Ricans, and yet there are coffee plantations as far as the eye can see.

ALAJUELA

(127 F2) (*∅ G5*) The altitude (950 m/ 3,117 ft) of the capital of the eponymous province maintains the spring-like climate all year round that its 52,000 inhabitants appreciate as much as visitors from the rest of the plateau.

There is much to discover: colonial flair in the four major cities, jungles and volcanoes in the national parks

Alajuela's pleasant atmosphere and convenient location close to the international airport is also increasingly appreciated by tourists. From the tiny church built by the Spanish in 1782 close to the settlement of La Lajuela has grown the country's second-biggest city and birthplace of the national hero Juan Santamaría, who served as a drummer boy in a war against US mercenaries in the 19th century. A large bronze memorial to him has been erected in the eponymous park south of the central park.

SIGHTSEEING

MUSEO HISTÓRICO CULTURAL JUAN SANTAMARÍA ●
A lavish building in the colonial style (north of the Parque Central), whose added watchtower recalls its former function as a prison, documents the battles between the US army of mercenaries under William Walker and the bold actions of the Costa Rican national hero. Pretty patio. *Tue–Sun 10am–5.30pm | admission free | C/ 2 Obispo*

priced on the stands at the *Mercado Municipal,* two blocks west of Central Park.

A vast sea of lights. Come to Pilas, about 7 km/4.4 mi away, in the evening to enjoy the panoramic views of the twinkling lights of San José and the surrounding villages. The food? Typical tico cuisine in huge portions. *N 712 | Pilas | tel. 24 41 93 47 | Moderate*

TACOBAR ALAJUELA
The breakfast bowls are eye-catchers, the juices and home-made lemonades fabulous. *C/ A 1 / Opposite C/ 11 | tel. 24 40 62 27 | Budget–Moderate*

SHOPPING

FERIA DEL AGRICULTOR
The ⊘ weekly market for fruit and vegetables, meat and fish is supplied by small and organic farmers, and also sells clothing, souvenirs and crafts. *Fri 2pm–9pm, Sat 7am–2pm | Plaza de Ferias | Av. 4 Concordia | www.plazaferias.com*

Award-winning coffee beans thrive on the slopes of Poás volcano

Tristán/Av. 1 | www.museojuansantama ria.go.cr

PARQUE CENTRAL
The centre of the city is the Parque Central, which is shaded by tall, dense mango trees and several impressive palm trees. Most of the other sights are within walking distance of the park. On the west side *(C 2)* are the National Bank and the building where the country's parliament first met in 1824. On the east side is the snowy-white *cathedral* from the turn of the last century, which has a vast corrugated metal dome.

FOOD & DRINK

Calle 1 in the centre is full of *sodas* and mid-class restaurants. Food is very well-

LEISURE & SPORTS

INSIDER TIP DOKA ESTATE ●
For over 90 years, the Vargas Ruíz family has had its coffee farm on the slopes of the volcano Poás, where it produces its choice, multiple-award-winning coffees. The roasting machine is a listed *architectural monument*, still used today and included in a guided tour. A pleasant highlight at the end is the *coffee tasting*, where you can also enjoy the family's own chocolates. *Tour daily 9am, 11am, 1.30pm, 2.30pm, 3.30pm | US$22 for 1½ hour tour | Sabanilla de Alajuela | 13 km/8.1 mi north-west of Alajuela | tel. 24 49 51 52 | www.doka estate.com*

WHERE TO STAY

LA ROSA DE AMERICA

Sweet, well-tended estate with a slightly old-fashioned charm. The highlight is the tropical garden with old trees and a refreshing pool. Airport shuttle on enquiry. *12 rooms | 1.7 km/1.1 mi east of Zoo Av. | tel. 24 33 27 41 | Budget*

PURA VIDA HOTEL

The main building and 650 ft² casitas with terraces are surrounded by banana trees and the giant bamboos of the former coffee plantation. The creative ⊕ organic food is produced by the Vietnam-born owner Nhi, while Berni will organise a hire car for you. Airport pick-ups provided. *6 rooms | Tuetal Sur corner Tuetal Norte | tel. 24 30 29 29 | www.puravida hotel.com | Moderate*

LOS ALEMANES

B&B at the foot of Poás Volcano with plain, well-tended rooms and a small pool in the tropical garden. *8 rooms | Carrillos de Poás | Ruta 118 al Poás | Alajuela (11 km/6.8 mi from the airport) | tel. 24 58 30 98 | Expensive*

INFORMATION

Although there is no tourist information office, the museum is pleased to provide assistance.

WHERE TO GO

POÁS (VOLCANO) ★ ● ⁓
(127 E–F1) (⑭ G4)

It made its presence felt again in 2017, when it briefly erupted and spewed sulphur, but it has calmed down again now. The road winds past coffee plantations and up to the National Park at 2,705 m/8,875 ft. Set off after an early breakfast (don't forget to take a jacket!), because clouds usually start to roll in during the morning, impairing the view of the massive 1.5-km/0.9 mi diameter

---

MARCO POLO HIGHLIGHTS

main crater. Sulphur vapours usually rise out of the turquoise waters of the lagoon. Then follow a jungle path that branches off just before the crater and is flanked by bromeliads and huge tree ferns to the *Laguna Botos*, a crater that became extinct several thousand years ago and is now a deep-blue lake. As an alternative to the expensive Poás restaurant: ☘ INSIDER TIP Two small restaurants with fabulous views and good prices a few kilometres from the entrance to the park. *Daily 8am–4pm | admission to the National Park US$15 (map of trails at the visitor centre)*

SARCHÍ (127 E1) (*∅ G5*)

The craft centre 30 km/18.6 mi away is famous for its hand-painted oxcarts *(carretas pintadas)*, which were once used to transport coffee and are now decorative items and a tourist attraction. There are lots of souvenir, craft and furniture shops in the small town. On the Calle Principal is the INSIDER TIP *Oxcart Factory* of Joaquín Chaverri, founded in 1902 and with a particularly large and colourful range of carts. A stay at ● ✺ *El Silencio Lodge & Spa (16 suites | tel. 24 76 03 03 | www.elsilenciolodge. com | Expensive)*, 13 km/8.1 mi north of Sarchí and surrounded by rainforest, is something you will never forget. Eco luxury is the apt characterisation of this intimate hotel, where guests stay in generous, loft-like *cabinas*. Three delicious meals at the restaurant, including Californian health cuisine, are the perfect complement to a stay – as well as a visit to the spa, where the attractions include yoga lessons. In Sarchí Norte is the 17.3-acre *Jardin Botánico Else Kientzler (daily 8am–4pm | www.ticoclub. com/kientzler.htm)*, unique with some 2,000 tropical plants – and the perfect spot for a picnic.

ZARCERO (127 E1) (*∅ F4*)

From Sarchí, head north-west for 20 km/ 12.4 mi to arrive at Zarcero, at a height of 1,736 m/5,696 ft. In the *Parque Evangelista Blanco Brenes* outside the church, an artist has trimmed cypress trees into over-sized fantasy shapes and figures *(topiarios)* – animals, but also helicopters and other objects. Excellent meals are served in the restaurant *Rancho de Ceci (2 km/1.2 mi north of the town in Laguna | tel. 24 63 33 44 | Moderate)*.

CARTAGO

(128 A2) (*∅ H5*) **Cartago, the former capital and the oldest city in the country, has often been challenged by fate: destroyed by six earthquakes (the worst ones were in 1841 and 1910), and threatened by eruptions from Irazú Volcano and floods.**

And yet, time and again Cartago, which was established by the Spanish in 1563, has been rebuilt, and until 1823 was the country's capital. Today the oldest city can be seen in an entirely new look, because all of the buildings are from the 20th century. Cartago (pop. 30,000) is 22 km/13.7 mi south-east of San José at 1,440 m/4,724 ft, so it is a little cooler here. Mountains and fertile plains surround the city, but a number of factories are also dotted around the green landscape.

SIGHTSEEING

BASÍLICA DE NUESTRA SEÑORA DE LOS ÁNGELES

Huge, bright white figures of angels watch over the main entrance. On 2 August the basilica, which was rebuilt in 1926 in the Byzantine style and is home to the shrine with the little Statue of St Mary, is the venue for a INSIDER TIP procession in the style of a folk festival, which thousands of people travel from all over the country to enjoy. There are numerous display cabinets inside the church, and believers make sacrifices in the form of miniature versions of

RUINAS DE LA PARROQUIA

Only the external walls of the parish church were spared by the serious earthquake of 1910; since then, the vast cathedral, constructed of granite in 1575, has been a ruin. The garden on the inside is open to visitors. *Daily 9am–5pm | admission free | Av. 2/C/ 2*

Angels watch over the Basílica de Nuestra Señora de Los Ángeles

their ailing organs and pray for healing. *Av. 2–4/C/ 16–18 | www.santuarion acional.org*

MUSEO HISTÓRICO-ETNOGRÁFICO ELÍAS LEIVA QUIRÓS ●

As well as archaeological finds from pre-Columbian times and anthropological and ethnographical exhibits, the museum also contains a large hall with weapons that belonged to the Spanish colonial rulers. *Mon–Fri 8am–2pm | admission free, donations gratefully accepted | C/ 3/Av. 3–5 | Edificio Norte, Colegio San Luis Gonzaga*

FOOD & DRINK

LA PUERTA DEL SOL

Typical *soda* with a bar and very busy from morning till night, ideal for checking out the local colour. *Av. 1/C/ 13 C | North side of the basilica | tel. 25 51 06 15 | restaurantelapuertadelsol.com | Budget*

SHOPPING

MERCADO MUNICIPAL

The market sells souvenirs and crafts such as ceramics and leather goods as well as food. *Mon–Sat 8am–6pm | Av. 1–3/C/ 2–4*

CARTAGO

LEISURE & SPORTS

INSIDER TIP LA FLOR DE PARAÍSO ⊙

Everyone on this beautiful, non-profit eco finca, which has been run by a charitable organisation for over 20 years, works with tremendous dedication. It's a great place for a Spanish course, to meet interesting people from all over the world, and to experience life on the farm (you are most welcome to join in!). Excursions and yoga courses are also on offer, and anyone who is interested in volunteering on the spur of the moment should just pop in. *La Flor, 7 km/4.4 mi northeast of Paraíso on Route 10 to Yas | www.la-flor.jimdo.org*

WHERE TO STAY

RIO PERLAS SPA & RESORT

You won't want to leave. Relax in the thermal waters of the large pool, explore the expansive tropical grounds, treat yourself to a massage, and then let yourself be lulled to sleep by the sounds of the jungle after dinner in the evening. Tip: the River Sound Suite. *64 rooms | Orosi de Cartago, 5 km/3.1 mi south of Cartago | 2 km/1.2 mi east of Puente Negro | tel. 25 33 33 41 | Moderate*

INFORMATION

There is no information centre, so call in at the Tourist Office in San José.

WHERE TO GO

GUAYABO ★ (128 B2) (*ω J5*)

20 km/12.4 mi north of Turrialba (gravel road), in the foothills of the eponymous volcano, lies this pre-Columbian excavation site, the most significant archaeological site in the country and a national monument. Guayabo was discovered back in the 19th century, but wasn't researched until the end of the 1960s. Roads, burial mounds, aqueducts and foundations all indicate that it was once a settlement that flourished between 800 and 1400, but was already inhabited in 500 BC. Art and cult objects made of ceramic, jade, gold and semi-precious stones all provide information on the cultural and religious significance of the place. So far, only a small area measuring approximately 200 x 100 m/656 x 328 ft of the over 494 acre ceremonial site has been reclaimed from the jungle. The rainforest is surrounded by paved paths. There are wonderful panoramic views from the ⚐ *Mirador*. Animal and plant-lovers enjoy the site's unspoilt flora and fauna. There is a map of the trails and excavation finds at the entrance to Guayabo, which is surrounded by dense forest. *Daily 8am–3.30pm | US$10*

IRAZÚ (VOLCANO) ★ ⚐
(128 A2) (*ω H5*)

The wind that blows from the edge of the crater of Irazú (3432 m/11,260 ft) is not only bitterly cold, but also opens up bird's-eye views of the country, of rich fields and small settlements. Exceptional: on clear days during the dry season (and only then), you can see two of the world's oceans at the same time, the coastline of the Gulf of Nicoya (Pacific) on one side, and the Caribbean coast of the Atlantic on the other. And Lake Nicaragua sparkles to the north. During the approach to the *National Park Volcán Irazú* 32 km/19.9 mi north-east of Cartago, there are lovely views of the mountain landscape of the Valle Central with potato and strawberry fields, oak groves and – not unusual in this area – herds of speckled Holstein dairy cows.

The vegetation stops shortly after you enter the park, leaving the area look-

Just one of over 750 species: orchid at the Jardín Lankester

ing uncannily like the moon – as Neil Armstrong himself once said on a visit. The ground is covered in fine, grey volcanic sand. Then, looking down into the 300 m/984 ft of the main crater, which measures 1,000 m/3,280 ft in diameter, is extremely impressive, even if the apple-green acid lake only contains water during the rainy season. If you walk north around the main crater, you'll come across several fumaroles. To the north-east is Turrialba Volcano, down in the valley to the west lies San José, and occasionally Barva Volcano rises up out of the clouds. On the way back you can enjoy the country's typical *gallo pinto* in various restaurants, served with fried bananas. Stay in the perfect location 7 km/4.4 mi north of Cartago, halfway to the volcano, at *Grandpa's Hotel (9 rooms | tel. 25 36 66 66 | www. grandpashotel.com | Budget–Moderate)* in lovely, well-kept *cabinas* with electric heaters and generous breakfasts. The

stylish neighbouring *Restaurante 1910 (Cot-Pacayas turning | Ctra. a Irazú | tel. 25 36 60 63 | www.restaurant1910. com | Moderate)* which has pictures of the eruption of 1910 and exceptionally good food is highly recommended (seabass: *corvina*, pork loin: *lomito). Park daily from 8am–3.30pm | US$15*

JARDÍN BOTÁNICO LANKESTER ★ ⊗ (128 A2) *(ⵜ H5)*

This botanic garden in an approximately 25-acre forest, which was planted by the English botanist Charles Lankester in the 1940s and is now maintained by the University of Costa Rica, is a must for orchid-lovers. Some of the over 750 varieties flower in the greenhouse. Forty types of bamboo, a large cactus garden, and countless migratory birds in winter. The botanic garden, which really is well worth a visit, has been extended to include a Japanese garden with a typical structure, bamboos, a pond and a bridge. An excellent time to visit is in March/April, when many of the orchids are in flower. *Daily from 8.30am–4.30pm | US$10 | 4 km/2.5 mi towards Paraíso | www.jbl.ucr.ac.cr*

TURRIALBA (128 B2) *(ω J5)*

The charming little town, which has a population of 40,000, is 37 km/23 mi to the east at an altitude of 625 m/2,050 ft in the foothills of Turrialba (3,339 m/10,955 ft) Volcano on the river of the same name.

charmingly restored by its Swiss owners. The riverside location encourages kayak rides, and excursions to the volcano and to Guayabo can be arranged.

VALLE OROSÍ (OROSÍ VALLEY) ★
(128 A2–3) *(ω H5–6)*

South-east of Cartago, travel through *Paraíso* (vast coffee plantations from there onwards) to a valley that is irrigated by the Río Grande de Orosí (later Reventazón). The river is dammed at

Adventure for wild water fans: rafting near Turrialba

It's a meeting place for white water fans, visitors to the volcano and amateur archaeologists on the way to Guayabo. Accommodation is available at the hotel INSIDER TIP ▶ *Casa Turire (16 rooms | La Suiza | from Turialba towards Guápiles/ La Suiza, turn right after 6 km/3.7 mi and again after 2 km/1.2 mi | tel. 25 31 11 11 | www.hotelcasaturire.com | Expensive)*, the loveliest plantation house in the area and

Cachí. Even the Spanish loved this area: in Orosí in 1735, the Franciscans built the little *mission church of San José*. The white bell tower stands beside the main building with its flat tiled gabled roof. Adjoining it is a small *museum of religious art (daily from 8am–noon, 1pm–5pm)*. The ☀ lookout point *Mirador Orosí* in the village offers lovely views of the charming valley.

In a pretty location on the south-east edge of the town is the ☙ *Tapantí Media Lodge (11 rooms | 2 km/1.2 mi towards Tapantí | www.hoteltapantimedia.wordpress.com | Budget)* with fabulous views (across the valley to the Turrialba Volcano), although the rooms are poor. It has Wi-Fi and a tennis court, and the Italian restaurant on the terrace on the first floor serves pizza and trout *(trucha)*. On the way from Orosí following the river and lake, about 10 km/6.2 mi past Cachí is the ● *Casa del Soñador* (The House of the Dreamer), a terrific woodworking studio. The artists here are totally committed to their craft: take a second look to see just what details the brothers Hermes and Miguel Quesada have carved into the wood! After crossing the high dam on the eastern shore of the lake, on the way back to Paraíso you'll come to *Ujarrás* (17 km/10.6 mi from Cartago) with the remains of a colonial *church,* built at the end of the 17th century. The ruins in a plantation were at risk of collapsing, and are now maintained by the Costa Rican tourist office ICT – and they're a great place for a picnic.

HEREDIA

(127 F2) *(ᗰ G5)* **Only 11 km/6.8 mi north of San José, and yet an entirely different world. Heredia scores with its balanced climate, colonial architecture and delightful small-town atmosphere – the perfect place to spend a few days.** The capital (pop. 75,000) of the eponymous province is Ciudad de Flores, the "City of Flowers", called that because of its spring-like temperatures, the containers of flowers outside the houses, the abundance of floral decorations. The tiled roofs of the white houses are dominated by the domes of the churches, cast-iron bars arch at the windows, massive wooden doors and thick walls keep the heat out and the houses cool, screening patios and gardens. The local industry is coffee, which is grown in the region. East of the centre is the national university, its students providing the atmosphere in the city. Heredia's layout is strictly colonial. It was founded by the Spanish in the first half of the 18th century, who came from the former capital Cartago, when they built a church.

LOW BUDGET

Costa Rica Backpackers **(U F3)** *(ᗰ f3)* *(110 beds | Av. 6/C/ 21–23 | Barrio California | San José | tel. 22 21 61 91 | www.costaricabackpackers.com)* is a *hostal* of hotel quality: large garden, pool, dormitories and double rooms, pleasant restaurant, salsa courses.

A brightly coloured guesthouse, a pleasant hotel with dormitory rooms or perhaps a *homestay*, i.e. stay with a family in pretty Orosí: *Montaña Linda (tel. 25 33 36 40 | www.montanalinda.com)* not only offers fabulous Spanish courses for not a lot of money, but also helps you find comfortable, inexpensive accommodation.

Surprise at the MADC, the *Museo de Arte y Diseño Contemporáneo* **(U E3)** *(ᗰ e3)* *(Mon–Sat 9.30am–5pm | Av. 3/C/ 15–17 | www.madc.cr)* in San José: one of the few old buildings in the capital is home to the biggest and best exhibition of contemporary art and painting. ● And admission is free on Mondays.

SIGHTSEEING

CASA DE LA CULTURA

The town-house of the former president Alfredo González Flores is now an office building and cultural centre with changing exhibitions and cultural performances in the evening. Some of the rooms in the building are also used as a history museum. *Av. Central Rafael Mora/C/ Central | North-east corner of the Parque Central | casadelaculturaalfredogonzalezflores.blogspot.com*

Fortified watch tower El Fortín in the centre of Heredia

EL FORTÍN

The town council is housed in parts of this Spanish fortress building, which includes a watch tower of 1876 with (inverted!) arrow slits. *Av. Central Rafael Mora | North side of the Parque Central*

LA INMACULADA CONCEPCIÓN

The city's earthquake-proof main church was completed in 1797 after a 30-year construction period with thick stone walls and 30 supporting columns inside. *Av. 2/C/ Central–1*

MUSEO DE BIOLOGÍA MARINA

The university's institute of marine biology has a museum with around 2,000 exhibits of flora and fauna from the country's oceans. *Mon–Fri 8am–noon, 1pm–4pm | admission free | Universidad Nacional | East end of the Av. Central*

INSIDER TIP MUSEO DE CULTURA POPULAR

Restored country house (1885) that illustrates rural life at the end of the 19th century. At the entrance are a vast stone oven and a stone tub for grinding coffee. On Sundays, the traditional restaurant *La Fonda (Budget)* near the museum is run by women from Heredia. *Sun 10am–5pm | US$2.50 | Santa Lucía de Barva | 4 km/2.5 mi north-east between Heredia and Barva de Heredia, 1.2 km/0.7 mi from the main street | www.museo.una.ac.cr*

PARQUE CENTRAL

Formerly the residences of wealthy coffee barons, mansions in the colonial and neoclassical style are grouped around the green heart of the city. On the north-west corner is the embellished post office, on the eastern side the vast church. *C/ Central/Av. Central–2*

FOOD & DRINK

EL TIGRE VESTIDO ⊗

The restaurant at the wonderful country estate *Finca Rosa Blanca* serves an excellent five-course dinner. They grow the organic ingredients themselves, and meals are accompanied by the best wines. Book in advance! *Santa Bárbara de Heredia | 5 km/3.1 mi to the northwest | tel. 22 69 95 55 | www.eltigreves tido.com | Expensive*

GRAN OPORTO

An elegant exterior and the corresponding ambience; excellent international cuisine, just the thing when you want a break from Costa Rican and Mexican food. The home-made cakes and gateaux are delicious. *Daily from 11.30am | Ctra. 111/C/28 | 300 m/984 ft west of Walmart | tel. 22 63 20 59 | Expensive*

L'ANTICA ROMA

Pasta al forno or a traditional stone-baked pizza? Accompanied by an excellent house wine, and to finish the *home-made strawberry cheesecake*. Muy rico! *Av. 7/Corner of Calle 7 | tel. 22 62 90 73 | Moderate*

SHOPPING

CENTRO COMERCIAL PASEO DE LAS FLORES

Two-storey shopping mall with over 300 shops, plus restaurants, cafés, bars, a cinema and a nightclub. *Mon–Sat 10.30am–9pm, Sun 11am–8pm | C/ Cordero | www.paseodelasflores.com*

LEISURE & SPORTS

FINCA CAFÉ BRITT

Heredia is all coffee! The town is surrounded by plantations, and the coffee finca is one of the best-known in the country. So what makes a gourmet coffee? Why are there huge tropical trees growing beside the coffee bushes? The entertaining hour-and-a-half tour *(Dec–April 9, 11, 1.15pm, 3.15pm, US$22)* of the coffee factory, which dates back to the 19th century, offers quite a few aha moments. Cocoa and nuts have also been marketed for a long time, and you can try them and buy them in the restaurant and shop *(daily from 8am–5pm). Mercedes Norte de Heredia (3 km/1.9 mi to the north) | www.coffee tour.com*

ENTERTAINMENT

There are several open-air concerts a week in the *pavilion* in the *Parque Central*. People meet in the bars on the west side of the university, and there are lots of students.

WHERE TO STAY

AMERICA

Modern hotel in a central location close to the Parque Central, basic rooms with air conditioning; the *El Rincón Tico* restaurant serves regional dishes. *42 rooms | C/ Central/Av. 2–4 | tel. 22 60 92 92 | www.hotelamericacr.com | Budget*

BOUGAINVILLEA

This hotel is equipped with a pool and tennis courts, a gym and a good lounge bar in the resort's landscaped park. The highlights in the rooms are the luxurious box spring beds. *81 rooms | Santo Tomás de Santo Domingo | 7 km/4.4 mi to the south-east | tel. 22 44 14 14 | www.hb.co.cr | Moderate*

CIBELES RESORT

Tall banana trees, palms and sweetly scented flowers, a pleasant pool, the large, well-kept American-style rooms a little fussy. Great price. *21 rooms | Extension Av. 13 to San Josecito | tel. 2 26 03 17 67 | Budget–Moderate*

Through the treetops in a steel basket: Rain Forest Aerial Tramway

nana plantations, is the town of Guápiles (pop. 20,000) from where there are hikes along the rivers and valleys of the north-east slopes of the Cordillera Central. On the way and 5 km/3.1 mi past the Río Sucio (right, 3 km/1.9 mi hiking trail with river crossing or rope bridge) is the legendary ★ ● *Rainforest Aerial Tramway (daily from 7.30am–2pm | US$65 / Bookings at the hotel or online | www.rainforestadventure.com)*, a gondola that takes you 1,300 m/4,265 ft into the rainforest and back in 90 minutes. The construction, which enabled the scientist Donald Perry to study the eco system in Rara Avis from above, is now also available to tourists. As well as the ride on the gondola, you can also book a bird-watching trip, a visit to the butterfly and ● frog garden(which includes the lucky *bluejeans dart frog*) or to the serpentarium, a canopy trip with seven zip lines, and treks. From Heredia: bus to Guápiles or Puerto Viejo de Sarapiquí *(hourly from C/ 12/Av. 7–9)* to the *Tramway (7 km/4.4 mi past the Zurquí tunnel)*.

INBIOPARQUE SANTO DOMINGO DE HEREDIA ● (127 F2) (𝄞 G5)

The park of the *Instituto Nacional de Biodiversidad* is a botanic garden, museum, research and teaching centre. ● The country's natural wonders are displayed and explained in two large halls. Teaching paths lead through the rainforest, dry and cloud forest to enclosures with iguanas, butterflies, caimans, frogs, snakes and many other animals. Video presentations and brochures provide further information. *Fri 9am–3pm, Sat/Sun 9am–4pm | guided walk with information (9am, 11am, 2pm) US$25 | 500 m/1,640 ft south of the Red Cross (cruz roja) of Santo Domingo and 250 m/820 ft east on the southern outskirts of the town | www.inbioparque.com*

Information is available at the Museo de Cultura Popular.

WHERE TO GO

GUÁPILES (125 D5) (𝄞 J4)

60 km/37.3 mi north-east of Heredia, on the road to Limón in the midst of ba-

PARQUE NACIONAL BRAULIO CARRILLO (127 F1) (*ω G–J 3–5*)

Steep mountains, gorges, rain and cloud forest: the large national park north of Heredia was created in 1978 when the new road from San José to Puerto Limón was constructed through it. The rainforest with 100 orchid varieties is a habitat for lots of animals – hundreds of birds, feline predators, tapirs, and the families of monkeys cannot be ignored! Rivers and waterfalls abound in the park, and the red flowers of large trees, *llama del bosque* (flame of the forest) glow. This is where the volcanoes *Barva* (2,906 m/9,534 ft, several crater lakes) and *Cacho Negro* are. Access to the Barva via San José de la Montaña to Sacramento, from there it's a 5-km/3.1-mi walk. The main entrance *Zurquí* (with a cafeteria and guide service) is on the National Route 32 from San José to Guápiles past the tunnel of the same name, and there are other entrances on the same road *(Puesto Carillo)* and on the turning to Puerto Viejo de Sarapiquí *(La Selva)*. *Daily 8am–3.30pm | US$12*

PUERTO VIEJO DE SARAPIQUÍ (124 C4) (*ω H3*)

To the north is a road that follows the Braulio Carrillo National park through some of Costa Rica's diverse landscapes and mountain regions to Puerto Viejo, 90 km/55.9 mi away and once an important port on the Rio Sarapiquí, which is connected to the Rio Colorado by the Río San Juan. This means that the Barra del Colorado and Tortuguero national parks are also accessible from Puerto Viejo by boat.

Accommodation tip: the *Posada Andrea Cristina (10 rooms | Ctra. a Virgen | Barrio El Jardín, 800 m/2,625 ft west of Puerto Viejo | tel. 27 66 62 65 | www.posadaandrea.wix.com/andreacristina | Budget)* is situated in a tropical garden. A good

choice at the centre of Puerto Viejo is the **INSIDER TIP** *Hotel El Bambú (40 rooms | Ctra. 505/opposite the Parque Principal | tel. 27 66 60 05 | www.elbambu.com | Budget)* with extremely spacious rooms and large verandas in a large park on stilts and with a large swimming pool. Very relaxing!

RARA AVIS (124 C4–5) (*ω H4*)

Amos Bien likens his private nature reserve to a fortress in the wilderness. On the north-east boundary of the Braulio Carrillo Park, a branch off the road to Puerto Viejo (access from Las Horquetas), lies Rara Avis, where the American biologist Donald Perry researched the rainforest canopy between 30 and 40 m/98.4 and 131.2 ft above the ground. Amidst the tangle of orchids, lianas and thousands of other epiphytes, a second nature world has established itself: it's home to snakes, frogs, insects and birds. Accommodation is available at the *Waterfall Lodge (tel. 27 64 11 11 | Moderate)*, a two-storey wooden building (no electricity!) that is surrounded by jungle and has a veranda and eight rustic double rooms. *Exciting ride to the hotel daily at 9am from the Rara Avis office Las Horquetas (15 km/9.3 mi, 3 hours) by tractor (US$200 per group) or horse (US$35 per person) | www.rara-avis.com*

SAN JOSÉ

MAP ON INSIDE BACK COVER
(127 F2) (*ω G–H5*) **San José is not a city to fall in love with. Due to the chequerboard layout of the roads, the combination of Spanish planning and modern extensions, dense traffic battles its way through while factories send their dirty fumes into the sky.**

SAN JOSÉ

CITY **WHERE TO START**
From the Coca Cola bus depôt it's a 1.5 km/0.9 mi walk along the Avenida Central to the **Plaza de la Cultura (U D–E3)** (*d–e3*). Taxis are not allowed to charge more than 1,370 colones. On the Plaza you will find an ICT Tourist Information centre, the gold museum and the Teatro Nacional. If you fancy a break, head to the café there or go and sit under the arcades of the Gran Hotel. The Avenida Central continues to the National Museum.

The city, which lies in a coffee valley at 1,150 m/3,773 ft at the foot of the Cordillera Central, has a population of around 440,000 (over 1.6 million if you include those in the outlying towns and villages). However, the location does mean the city has a pleasant climate. San José has been the capital since 1823, and is a modern, very prosperous metropolis with only a few magnificent buildings and remains from the Spanish era. Attempts have been made to add a few spots of colour to the grey city. The neoclassical Hotel del Rey and the wooden houses from the turn of the last century in the old quarter of Barrio Amón now shine in new splendour, as do the Parque Morazán, Parque de la Merced and Parque Central.

SIGHTSEEING

As in many towns and cities in Costa Rica, the Avenidas run east to west (the odd ones are to the north of the Avenida Central, the evens to the south), the Calles from north to south (odds to the east of the Calle Central, evens to the west).

The prettiest area is Barrio Amón just north of the centre, with well-cared-for wooden houses in the Caribbean style and Victorian buildings from the colonial times – perfect for a stroll.

MUSEO DEL ORO PRECOLOMBINO ★
● **(U D–E3)** (*d–e3*)

The gold treasure is in the cellar: the hoard in the underground museum complex of the Banco Central is not only of inestimable value, but is also fascinating and beautiful. Tiny, ancient frogs, birds and crocodiles, thousands of years old and made of pure gold; little, highly detailed dancers and shaman, fabulous necklaces and bracelets, plates and goblets – the 1,600 items on display date back to between 500 BC and the 16th century. These treasures alone are worth a visit to the hectic city of San José. *Daily from 9am–5pm | US$12 (including coin museum on the top floor) | C/ 5/Av. Central | below the Plaza de la Cultura | www.museosdelbancocentral.org*

MUSEO NACIONAL ★ **(U E3)** (*e3*)

Typical Costa Rica. The tour of the National Museum starts in a butterfly house full of palm trees and tropical flowers. There's flapping and buzzing all around. It is interesting as you continue: you can see the Nobel Peace Prize awarded to Óscar Arias Sánchez as well as the office and original furniture of former presidents. Fabulous: the roof garden with frangipani trees and benches to sit on – perfect for a rest. *Tue–Sun 8.30am–4.30pm | US$9 | Plaza de la Democracia | C/ 15/Av. Central–2 | www.museocostarica.go.cr*

MUSEO NACIONAL DEL JADE
(U E2) (*e2*)

You won't see a larger exhibition of pre-Columbian excavations, stones and figures made of jade anywhere else. Even though public opinion of the new building, which cost more than US$20 million and looks like a chunk of uncut jade, is on the negative side: on the inside, the lights are dimmed and over its five floors (!), you are immersed in the whole world of this precious gem that was once appreciated all over Central America for its use in cult actions. INSIDER TIP The little sculptures by the local sculptor Olger Villegas Cruz in the entrance hall (admission is free) look surprisingly alive. *Daily 10am–5pm | US$15 | Av. Central/C/ 13 | west side of the Plaza de la Democracia | www.museodeljadeins.com*

PARQUE NACIONAL (U E–F3) (*m e–f3*)
There is an eye-catching bronze monument of 1885 in the middle of the very central park that marks the abolition of slavery and the fact that five Central American states resisted William Walker's attempts at annexation. *Av. 1–3/ C/ 15–17*

PARQUE ZOOLÓGICO SIMÓN BOLÍVAR (U E2) (*m e2*)
A visit to the zoo in Costa Rica? Here the vast green surroundings with tropical trees and a lake are more reminiscent of a botanic garden – a refreshing antidote to the looming attack of big city rage. Apart from the jaguars and turtles, the *ticos* are most fascinated by the boa constrictors. *Daily 9am–4.30pm | 2,600 colones | Av. 11/C/ 7–9 | www.fundazoo.org*

TEATRO NACIONAL ★
(U D–E3) (*m d–e3*)
The neo-Renaissance theatre of 1897 was based on the Paris Opera, and with its marble staircases and frescoes, gilded foyer and Venetian mirrors, it is the loveliest theatre in Central America. The ceiling painting in the entrance hall can be

Museo Nacional del Jade: jewellery and ceramics from pre-colonial times

seen on the 5 colon note. The auditorium, which tilts towards the stage, is levelled for dance performances. The best place in San José for good coffee and cake is the fabulous ● *Belle Époque Café (Mon–Sat 9am–7pm, Sun 9am–6pm | tel. 20 10 11 19 | www.almadecafe.cr). Tue–Sun 9am–5pm | US$10 | Av. Segunda/C/ 3–5 | www.teatronacional.go.cr*

FOOD & DRINK

KALÚ (U E3) (📖 e3)

Real artists are at work here, creating everything from salads with sweet potato fries to chocolate gateau with custard and nut croquant: every dish in this hip meeting place is an eye-catcher. Chic garden area. *Calle 31/Av. 5 | Barrio Escalante | tel. 22 53 84 26 | Moderate*

SODA TAPIA (U A3) (📖 a3)

For 80 years *gallo pinto* has been served in La Sabana near the Museum of Art. It's lively, and occasionally gets loud, on the roadside terrace. *C/ 42/Av. 2 | tel. 22 22 67 34 | Budget*

TIN JO (U E4) (📖 e4)

Asian cuisine: Indian and Thai curries, fish specialities and seafood, lots of vegetarian dishes; extensive wine list. *C/ 11/Av. 6–8 | tel. 22 21 76 05 | www.tinjo.com | Moderate*

VISHNU (U D3) (📖 d3)

Chains of vegetarian restaurants. The Dish of the Day *(comida corrida)*, is popular, and served quickly. *Av. 1/C/ 1–3 | tel. 22 56 60 63 | Budget*

SHOPPING

As a general rule, the goods on offer on the capital's markets and in the craft stores are largely from Guatemala and South America. However, there are also various pretty, typically Costa Rican products. One treasure trove – especially at weekends – is the *Plaza de la Cultura* (U D–E3) (📖 d–e3) *(Av. Central/C/ 5)* with stands where people haggle for hammocks, ceramics, wood carvings and leather goods. At the foot of the National Museum on the *Plaza de la Democracia* (U E3) (📖 e3), small stands sell woven goods from Guatemala and silver and ceramics from Mexico.

LEISURE & SPORTS

CRUZ DE ALAJUELITA ☄ (127 F2) (📖 G5)

Ready for some action? San José is surrounded by mountains, and there is a relaxing walk up Cerro San Miguel (2,036 m/6,680 ft, and visible on clear days). On the Avenida 2, take the bus outside the church La Merced to the suburb of Alajuelita El Llano, and start walking there – it will take you between two and three hours. Although the trail is not marked, the large cross on the top of the mountain will show you the way. Cafés and bars with lookout terraces *(miradores)* of the lavish countryside fringe the route.

ENTERTAINMENT

Electronic, reggae, hip hop: *Club Vertigo (Thu 9pm–2.30am, Fri/Sat 9pm–6am | Paseo Colón | Centro Colón | vertigocr.com)* is the biggest and best location for partying. The continent's best-known DJs spin the turntables, and there are two dance floors.

WHERE TO STAY

The loveliest spot is the atmospheric, popular quarter *Barrio Amón* north of the (noisy) centres, where there are lots of B&Bs in traditional buildings, most of the individual and cosy.

ALTA ☄ (0) (📖 0)

Modern hacienda style in the hills to the west with views of San José. Rooms, service and restaurant are all excellent. Highly recommended: booking with airport collection. *23 rooms | Los Altos de las Palomas | tel. 22 82 41 60 | www.the altahotel.com | Expensive*

BALMORAL (U E3) *(ⓂⓄ e3)*

Four stars and a modern façade and top location in the historic centre. The large restaurant café with plenty of atmosphere is a popular meeting place; regular live music. *112 rooms | Av. Central/C/ 7–9 | tel. 22 22 50 22 | www.balmoral. co.cr | Moderate*

INSIDER TIP ► COSTA RICA GUESTHOUSE (U F3) *(ⓂⓄ f3)*

Stylish and inexpensive: there are large, differently furnished rooms in an old colonial house of 1905 (some have shared bathrooms). Pleasant patios and Internet. *25 rooms | Av. 6/C/ 21–23 | tel. 22 23 70 34 | www.costa-rica-guesthouse. com | Budget*

COSTA RICA MARRIOTT SAN JOSÉ

The location outside the city is worthwhile. Views of the surrounding mountains, fabulous colonial architecture on an old plantation, pools and a spa that is all about coffee, perfect for pampering. Free airport pick-up. *299 rooms | 700 m/2,297 ft west of Bridgestone/Firestone | La Ribera de Belen | tel. 22 98 00 00 | Expensive*

INFORMATION

INSTITUTO COSTARRICENSE DE TURISMO (ICT) (0) *(ⓂⓄ 0)*

The main ICT office has information on the entire country and San José. Branch on the Av. Central next to the entrance to the casino of the Grand Hotel (near the Plaza de la Cultura). *Autopista General Cañas 1 | east side of Juan Pablo II bridge, Uruca | tel. 22 99 58 00 | www. visitcostarica.com*

Still buzzing at dusk: San José

THE NORTH-WEST

Farm, zebu cattle and *sabaneros*, the Central American cowboys on horseback, create the picture of the "Wild West". Costa Rica's North-West is a hot and dry region.

People here live from cattle breeding, and the land is covered by pastures and steppes. The North-West consisting of the province Guanacaste (the second biggest in the country) and partly of Puntarenas is one of the least touristically developed regions. Its vast plains with parched grass is reminiscent of the African savannahs, the only shade being provided by the umbrella-like trees. The only rain worth mentioning falls between May and November, and the area soon turns a fresh green. By the same token, the region has over a dozen parks and reservations with

tropical dry forests and rainforests in the low plains, mist-enshrouded in higher regions. Ocean turtles appreciate the still largely empty coastal sections as a breeding ground.

LIBERIA

(122 C3) (*Ø C3*) **During the summer months, heat and dust cover the light tufa-plastered roads and white houses, which gave Liberia the name "Ciudad Blanca" – white town.**

But now most of the white has been covered in asphalt and grey plaster. With a population of 48,000 (and a further 10,000 in the surrounding municipalities), the capital of the province

Cowboy romance, tropical beaches and numerous national parks await in the "Wild West" and the Pacific coast

of Guanacaste was founded in 1769 on the banks of the Río Liberia in a chequerboard pattern, and is a rather placid town, a shopping and entertainment destination at the weekends for the *sabaneros* working on the cattle and horse farms in the region. Liberia's location on the Carretera Interamericana, as the Pan-American Highway is called in Costa Rica, not only brings through traffic to the town, but is also a starting point for visits to the Nicoya Peninsula with its popular beaches and to the na-

tional parks Santa Rosa and Rincón de la Vieja to the north.

SIGHTSEEING

SUN DOORS

Many of the houses have the *puerta del sol* that is typical of the town. Two outside doors lead into the houses from the north-east and the north-west. In bygone days, the door facing the sun was left open so light could come in; today, now that there is electricity, the door facing away

LIBERIA

from the sun stands open to let fresh air in while the heat remains outside.

FOOD & DRINK

EL BRAMADERO

For over 50 years, people here have known how to prepare a juicy steak. Locals and newcomers sit at long tables to enjoy the barbecued meals. Vegetarians are happy with the generous salads and freshly prepared vegetable dishes. *Daily | Panamericana/Av. 1 | next to McDon-*

LEISURE & SPORTS

PONDEROSA ADVENTURE PARK

This private animal reserve is home to elephants, giraffes and zebras, and you can enjoy the safari atmosphere on a wildlife tour with the ranger. Another fabulous experience is riding out on the beautifully cared-for horses. *Daily 9am–5pm | Safari tour US$50 | El Salto, Pan-American Highway, 8 km/5 mi south of Liberia | tel. 22 88 10 00 | www.ponderosaadven turepark.com*

Perfectly formed: you can see Arenal Volcano from a distance

ald's | tel. 26 66 03 71 | www.hotelbrama dero.com | Moderate

EL CAFÉ LIBERIA

"As time goes by" atmosphere in a wonderful colonial house. As well as the best tico cuisine, it also serves classics such as Caesar's Salad and pasta, coffee specialities and rich desserts and cake. Excellent on every level. *Casa Zuñiga | C/ Real | tel. 26 65 16 60 | www.cafeliberia. com | Budget*

WHERE TO STAY

BOYEROS

Very pleasant with pools in a comfortable location and greenery, balcony rooms. *70 rooms | Pan-American Highway/Av. 2–4 | tel. 26 66 07 22 | www.hotelboyeros.com | Moderate*

HOTEL LIBERIA

This colonial-style building from the 1940s has been skilfully restored. Ask for a room in the old building (casona), they cost about the same and have a fabulous atmosphere – *muy elegante*! *18 rooms | C/ Central | tel. 26 66 01 61 | www.hotel liberiacr.com | Budget*

LAS ESPUELAS

Modern, comfortable rooms surrounding a large pool. The pool bar is the place to meet in the evenings, and there are occasional folklore performances. Restaurant with a rustic interior, famed for its seafood. *44 rooms | Pan-American Highway (2 km/1.2 mi south of the Liberia turning) | tel. 26 66 01 44 | Moderate*

INFORMATION

Information on the town is available from *liberiacostaricainfo.com* and *www.muniliberia.go.cr*, and on the province from *www.guanacastecostarica.com*.

WHERE TO GO

LAGUNA DE ARENAL (LAKE ARENAL) (123 E3–4) ($\varnothing$ D–E3)

The 40-km/24.9-mi long reservoir is one of the best inland surfing spots in the world. Constant trade winds (at their strongest between January and April) come courtesy of the funnel-like, 1,633 m/5,358 ft ★ *Volcán Arenal* east of the lake. The view of the active volcano from the south-west bank or the Parqueo Interior (3 km/1.9 mi west) is fabulous in good weather, when you can see the perfect cone shape of the volcano against the clear sky. Surfers meet on the west shore at the INSIDERTIP *Tico Windsurf – Kitesurf & SUP Center (www.ticowind.com)*; also surfboard hire. There are also various restaurants and cottages on the west shore. We recommend the ✶ INSIDERTIP *Volcano Lodge (65 rooms | Ctra. La Fortuna–Tabacón | tel.*

24 79 28 00 | www.volcanolodge.com | *Expensive*) on the La Palma river with comfortable rooms and views of the volcano, transport to the hot springs and the volcano.

In La Fortuna you will find the hotel *La Fortuna (44 rooms | Av. 325/C/ 466 | tel. 24 79 91 97 | www.lafortunahotel. com | Budget–Moderate)* just a block from the central Plaza. This rather unappealing, modern, multi-storey building has great views of the volcano and well-maintained rooms at good prices. There is also a small restaurant. *La Choza Inn (16 rooms | Av. 331 | La Fortuna | tel. 24 79 90 91 | www.lachozainnhostel. com | Budget)* is extremely good value,

★ Volcán Arenal
None of the volcanoes on Costa Rica reaches up so perfectly → p. 53

★ Balnearios in La Fortuna
Swimming pool with thermal waters at 45 °C/113 °F and views of Arenal Volcano → p. 54

★ Parque Nacional Rincón de la Vieja
Hot springs, crater lakes and a pool with healthy volcanic mud → p. 54

★ Reserva Bosque Nuboso Santa Elena
Educational trails through the jungle without the crowds → p. 58

★ Skywalk in Monteverde
A walk amongst the treetops 40 m/131.2 ft up → p. 59

MARCO POLO HIGHLIGHTS

and more like a small hotel than a hostel. In La Fortuna and the surrounding area are several ⭐ *thermal pools*: Arenal Volcano provides water at 45 °C/113 °F with beneficial minerals, and the spring is constantly replenishing the pool with new water. The *Balneario Tabacón* 12 km/7.5 mi from La Fortuna belongs to the luxury hotel *Tabacón Grand Spa Thermal Resort (www.tabacon.com)* and is the best address for wellness and relaxation in the hot spring water. A *day pass* costs US$85 (including lunch, US$94 in peak season). Rainforest vegetation and a dozen pools styled with huge rocks are the key feature of the *Baldi Hot Springs (www. baldicostarica.cr | daily 10am–10pm)* at the resort of the same name, approx. 4 km/2.5 mi west of La Fortuna, a *day pass* costs US$34. The ● *Eco Termales La Fortuna (US$32 (4 hours) | opposite Baldi | tel. 24 79 87 87 | www.ecotermales-for tuna.cr)* are open daily from 9am until 9pm, and have five pools. Maximum 100 guests at the same time, booking recommended. The INSIDER TIP *Termales Los Laureles (www.termalesloslaureles.com)* with four pools are 7 km/4.4 mi west of La Fortuna, and the best value for money at US$12 for admission.

● *The Springs Resort & Spa (www.spring scostarica.com)* is situated on a huge tropical estate 13 km/8.1 mi north-west of La Fortuna. The main building with large, luxurious rooms and suites is surrounded by 18 pools and thermal pools, some with spectacular views of the volcano, and one of the best spas in the country. Admission for day visitors US$40. Up for some thrills? Then get yourself to the ❧ INSIDER TIP *Puentes Colgantes (daily 7.30am–4.30pm | US$26 | La Fortuna, 4 west of Tabacón, turning at the reservoir, then 2 km/1.2 mi along a well-made road | https://misticopark.com/self-guided-hanging-bridges):* a 3-km/1.9-mi trail

that can be quite a challenge because it is frequently interrupted by numerous hanging bridges up to 100 m/328 ft long, including several that are quite adventurous. Lovely view of Arenal Volcano and the Cordillera Central; restaurant. South of the lake is the ● ❧ *Butterfly Conservatory (daily 8.30am–4.30pm | US$14.50 | get here from the reservoir approx. 7 km/4.4 mi along the east shore on a gravel road | www.butterflyconser vatory.org)* with views of the lake and the volcano. Tropical butterflies flutter about the butterfly house, next door frogs croak in the ranarium, and you'll smell the medicinal herbs on a walk through the rainforest.

The *Arenal Natura Ecological Park (daily 8am–5pm | US$29 | www.arenalnatu ra.com)* is on the road from La Fortuna to the volcano (6 km/3.7 mi), 300 m/984 ft north-east of the *Volcano Lodge*. Two-hour guided tour with lots of information on around 25 frog and toad species, all in lovely terrariums; also a number of snakes and crocodiles.

Some 2.5 km/1.6 mi east of La Fortuna (towards San Carlos, bus station Agua Azul) is the 🌐 *Ecocentro Danaus (daily 8am–5pm | US$13 | www.ecocentro danaus.com)*, a private, enthusiastically run, multiple award-winning conservation area. INSIDER TIP The 90-minute tours and the opportunity to meet Malekus, members of a small indigenous tribe. Some 50 km/31.1 mi from La Fortuna, they live from agriculture and fishing, and come here to sell their hand-made bows and arrows and balsa wood sculptures. One of the rare opportunities to meet the Malekus, who (also) speak Spanish.

PARQUE NACIONAL RINCÓN DE LA VIEJA ⭐ (122 C2) (*ω C2*)

27 km/16.8 mi north-east of Liberia, the nature park surrounds the volcano

This is the life: pool in La Fortuna that is fed by a hot spring

(1,895 m/6,217 ft) of the same name and one other one (Santa María, 1,916 m/6,286 ft). In the geothermally active forest with over 250 birds species, sulphur and other hot springs bubble up, and you'll see fumaroles and crater lakes. Over 30 streams and rivers have their source in the park, and there are the most diverse vegetation zones between 600 and 1,900 m/1,968 and 6,234 ft in altitude. The Rincón Volcano has erupted in several places, most recently in 1995. Excursions are offered from Liberia (on a new tarmacked road. *Park Tue–Sun 8am–4pm | US$15*

Stay in lovely surroundings with waterfalls and views of the volcano at the ⊛ ⋇ *Hacienda Guachipelin (54 rooms | 5 km/3.1 mi north of Liberia, then 17 km/10.6 mi east, at the entrance to the national park | tel. 26 90 29 00 |* www.guachipelin.com | *Moderate):* cattle ranch, stud farm and eco lodge in one, ideal for active guests as it also offers a wide range of sporting activities. **INSIDERTIP** Six pools with healing volcanic mud (5 km/3.1 mi from the hotel) to boost your health.

BEACHES (122 A–B3) (*Ø A–B 2–3*)
Beach combers and sun-worshippers are spoilt for choice: there are countless developed beaches some 20 km/12.4 mi west of Liberia. First you arrive at the Papagayo Peninsula. There are around 30 tiny beaches and bays along the 25-km/15.5-mi steep coast. The region became famous for discerning luxury holidays with the opening of the *Four Seasons Resort Papagayo (155 rooms | tel. 26 96 00 00 | www. fourseasons.com/cos tarica | Expensive).*

Accommodation for horse-lovers: Hacienda Guachipelin, a combination of ranch and eco lodge

The amount of grace and perfection that went into planning this complex is impressive, from the 7-km/4.4-mi long drive through tropical gardens, to the comfortably furnished rooms and suites with bamboo and rattan.

By contrast, the *Apartamentos Casa Lora* (tel. 26 70 06 42 | www.casalora.com | *Moderate*) offers four-star luxury at very good prices. The two apartments (377 ft²) and three holiday homes (753 ft² on two storeys) are situated among palm trees and banana trees; kitchenette and terrace. At sundown, guests meet between the pool and the pavilion for a beer. The centre of the old fishing village with several restaurants and shops is 1.5 km/0.9 mi away on the beach.

7 km/4.4 mi further, north of the Papagayo Peninsula, the *Playa Hermosa* with sparkling blue water that gently laps the bay with soft ways, lives up to its name of "Lovely beach".

MONTEVERDE

(123 E4) *(Ø E4)* Monteverde is an extensive range of cloud forests at 1,300–1,800 m/4,265–5,906 ft, where several government, communal and private nature reserves have been opened. You can visit them from the main town of Santa Elena (pop. 6,000) on an organised tour, by hire car or by bus.

A dozen North American Quaker families came here in the 1950s and founded the settlement of Monteverde and the farm. The 741 acre rainforest Reserva Bosque Nuboso Santa Elena (*www. reservasantaelena.org*) is the responsibility of the commune. It contains numerous *trails*, some paved hiking trails. The private Monteverde Cloud Forest Biological Reserve, maintained by the international research group *Centro Científico Tropical (www.cct.*

or.cr), is 6 km/3.7 mi east of Santa Elena (bus link). The reserve, which originally measured only 1.2 mi², now covers an area of 19.3 mi². The so-called children's rainforest (Bosque Eterno de los Niños) is maintained by a successful (private) nature conservation organisation; it also has numerous hiking trails *(sendero, trail)*. Santa Elena can only be reached by 4-wheel drive. Average temperatures around 18 °C/64 °F and frequent rain, so bring a rain jacket and hiking boots.

SIGHTSEEING

BOSQUE ETERNO DE LOS NIÑOS (BEN) (CHILDREN'S ETERNAL RAIN FOREST) ●

A rainforest for children! Only in Costa Rica: children from 44 nations donated money to start up the country's biggest nature reserve – an amazing 87 mi². Their dream came true, and today schools around the world collect money for the Bosque Eterno. The organisation is also always on the lookout for young volunteers (18 and over) to help run tourist groups or to work in the rainforest *(https://www.engageglobally.org/)*. The Sendero Bajo de Tigre (3.5 km/2.2 mi) is one of the trails that is signposted for hikers, and although there are hardly any feline predators you may well encounter monkeys, toucans and coati – and perhaps even the occasional sloth. *Daily 8am–5pm | US$20 | Estación Biológica San Gerardo, 7 km/4.4 mi north-east of Santa Elena | www.acmcr.org*

EL TRAPICHE

This old-fashioned sugar mill with a patio restaurant still produces sugar cane juice today. You'll see so much on a two-hour tour of the farm, and things are explained in a really interesting and exciting way. Juan Hidalgo and his family also grow coffee here, then roast the beans

RODEO COSTA RICAN-STYLE

Lots of horses are broken in on the many ranches in the region around Liberia, and rodeos take place to provide entertainment with men riding wild bulls. The highlight is 25th July, when there are cattle shows and rodeos on the *Día de Guanacaste*. There are also rodeos in the first week of September to mark the *Semana Cultural*.

Treetop trail with a sky-high name: Skywalk at the Santa Elena Reserve

and produce fabulous gourmet coffee. *Muy simpático!* INSIDER TIP Travel to the last stop in an oxcart: fine chocolate is made from cocoa beans. *Tours daily at 10am and 3pm, Sun at 3pm only | US$32 | 2 km/1.2 mi north-west of Santa Elena | www.eltrapichetour.com*

JARDÍN DE MARIPOSAS (BUTTERFLY GARDEN)

Scared of spiders? These specimens in turquoise and green will soon cure your phobia. And of course, there are plenty of butterflies as well. The American founder is a taxonomist, so there are four strictly divided enclosures. It's fascinating to be in the *rearing chamber* – the nursery, if you like – and be fortunate enough to see a butterfly that has just emerged from its cocoon. *Daily 8.30am–4pm | US$15 with a tour | turn right off the Santa Elena–Monteverde road | www.monteverdebutterflygarden.com*

RESERVA BOSQUE NUBOSO SANTA ELENA (SANTA ELENA CLOUD FOREST RESERVE) ★

Schoolchildren in the town and Canadian helpers created this small, not too busy reserve with courses for biology students and several kilometres of educational paths. Here too, rain and the constant mist from the clouds transform the forests into a bizarre fairy-tale world. INSIDER TIP If you're really lucky, you might even spot the mythical quetzal, identifiable by its metres-long tail feathers. *Daily 7am–4pm | US$14 | 7 km/4.4 mi north-east of Santa Elena | www.reservasantaelena.org*

SELVATURA ADVENTURE PARK

In this private cloud forest (1.9 mi²), hanging bridges take you through the treetops *(Tree Top Walkways)*, there is a *Butterfly* and *Hummingbird Garden* and an *insect museum*. Many enjoy the thrill of the *Canopy Tour*, which consists of 15 zip lines that take you some 3 km/1.9 mi into the cloud forest (about 2 1/2 hours). *Canopy tours US$50 | 7 km/4.4 mi northeast of Santa Elena next to the San Gerardo Forest Reserve | www.selvatura.com*

SKYWALK ★

Wow! Six hanging bridges combine in a 500-m/1,640-ft path through the 40-m/131.2-ft high treetops of the cloud forest! A perfectly safe adventure for children, too. *Also guided tours daily 7.30am, 9.30am, 11.30am, 1.30pm | US$39 | 3.5 km/2.2 mi towards the Santa Elena Reserve | www.skyadventures.travel*

FOOD & DRINK

BESO ESPRESSO

This is a great place to relax and enjoy! With one (or more) of the nine coffee varieties that are mostly freshly roasted, and prepared in the professional express machine or filtered, whichever you prefer. Lovely atmosphere. The cakes, brownies and muffins are also delicious. *Daily | Ctra. 606 | Santa Elena | Beside the taxi rank | tel. 26 45 68 74*

SABOR TICO

The *casado* – rice, beans, fried plantain and warm tortillas – is delicious, as are the other plain dishes that are served up at excellent prices. Lovely view of the town from the ☀ terrace. *Daily | Ctra. 620 | Santa Elena | Opposite the football pitch | tel. 26 45 58 27 | www.restaurante sabortico.com | Moderate*

INSIDER TIP TAQUERÍA TACO TACO

You might be able to discover the secret of these delicious tacos: better try one quickly! There are no seats. If you want to sit down, you'll have to find somewhere on the hostel terrace next door. *Daily from noon | Ctra. 606 | Santa Ele-*

na | Next door to the Pensión Santa Elena | tel. 26 45 79 00 | Budget

SHOPPING

CASEM

The souvenir shop of the Women's Cooperative sells hand-made wooden toys, wall carpets, ⊛ eco T-shirts and excellent Monteverde coffee. *Daily 8am–5pm | On the road between Santa Elena and the park entrance opposite Stella's Bakery | www.casemcoop.blogspot.com*

LA LECHERÍA

The renowned Quaker cheese factory *(fábrica de queso)* is open to the public. Self-caterers aren't the only one who appreciate the 17 cheese varieties and dairy products. INSIDER TIP Be sure to try the smooth chocolate ice cream with candied fruits! *Mon–Sat 7.30am–4pm | Tours 9am and 2pm | US$12 | on the Santa Elena–Monteverde road, 300 m/984 ft southeast Casem | www.monteverdecheese factory.com*

IGUANA

Although the *iguana* is considered a delicacy in El Salvador and Mexico, it is not consumed so much in Costa Rica. The reptile, which looks not unlike a small dragon, can grow up to 2 m/6.6 ft in length, but is peaceful and not at all dangerous – it will run away if you approach it. You'll see them everywhere, not just in the national parks, but on hotel sites as well. Their favourite activity is to lie absolutely still in trees. The population appreciates the iguana because it keeps rats and mice at bay.

LEISURE & SPORTS

A number of stables provide horses so you can explore the area on horseback. INSIDER TIP *Sabine's Smiling Horses (2 km/1.2 mi south of Santa Elena on the road to San José | tel. 83 85 24 24 | www. smilinghorses.com)* offers hacks through the rainforest for US$45 (2½ hours).

WHERE TO STAY

You'll find basic accommodation in Santa Elena, mid-class hotels on the road from Santa Elena to Monteverde.

ARCO IRIS LODGE ⬥⬥

The wood-clad casitas, also with four-bed rooms, adapt beautifully to the jungle, and after sunset you can watch the glow worms on your own terrace. The Honeymoon Bungalow has a four-poster bed and other frills. *20 rooms | Santa Elena | tel. 26 45 50 67 | www.arcoirislodge.com | Moderate*

EL BOSQUE

Basic, clean rooms with a bathroom, arranged around a large green area. Hiking trails, camping facilities, good restaurant. *29 rooms | on the Santa Elena–Monteverde road, 2.5 km/1.6 mi before the park and 100 m/328 ft west of Casem | tel. 26 45 51 58 | www.hotel elbosquecr.com | Budget*

HELICONIA

Stylish wood look, on a hill, with a spa and Italian restaurant. *55 rooms | Cerro Plano, between Santa Elena and Monteverde | tel. 26 45 66 16 | www.hotelhelico nia.com | Moderate*

INSIDER TIP LAS ORQUIDEAS

Small feel-good hotel, well-tended chalet style rooms, breakfast included, communal kitchen for guests and a large balcony out to the cloud forest. The Costa Rican owners offer valuable tips for excursions in the area. *8 rooms | 300 m/984 ft south Santa Elena | tel. 26 45 55 09 | www.orquideasmonteverde.com | Budget–Moderate*

INFORMATION

ASOCIACIÓN CONSERVACIONISTA MONTEVERDE
Cerro Plano (opposite Jardín de Mariposas) | tel. 26 45 50 03 | www.montever deinfo.com | www.acmcr.org

PENÍNSULA DE NICOYA (NICOYA PENINSULA)

The darker skin of the natives is a testimony to the ancestors of the cattle breeders who once settled on the peninsula: Chorotega Indians.

They also gave the peninsula its name, "Land surrounded by water on both sides", because it reached out about 100 km/62 mi into the ocean. There are numerous attractive, sleepy, isolated and lively beaches all around the peninsula. Tourists and locals alike appreciate the beaches and bays on the Pacific side.

Take plenty of time with you, because not many of the roads are tarmacked, and travelling them is quite an adventure. However, the beach that is served by only one bus a day is often the loveliest. You'll find accommodation in all classes on the beaches, from a hot-and-humid boarding house room in the middle of the town to an air-conditioned bungalow with ocean views.

INFORMATION

ICT TOURIST OFFICE

Ctra. a Sámara, southern exit from Nicoya, opposite the university | tel. 26 85 32 60

WHERE TO GO ON NICOYA

GUAITIL AND SANTA CRUZ (122 B5) (*B4*)

The tiny town of *Guaitil* (10 km/6.2 mi east of Santa Cruz, which you get to on Route 21 north of Nicoya) is known as the centre of ceramic production. Lots of hotels decorate their foyers with the bulbous vases in the pre-Columbian style. The vases, jugs and pots are fired by Indian families in clay-walled ovens.

On the way back, it's worth stopping off at the small town of *Santa Cruz* (pop. 15,000), the self-styled "Folklore capital" of the country. The music tradition, which is practised all year round, has its highlight at the middle of January, when old dances are performed and costumed dancers proceed through the town. Local specialities are served at the *sodas* around the town park. You'll find accommodation at the *La Calle de Alcalá (28 rooms | C/ de Alcalá/Av. 7 | tel. 26 80 00 00 | www.hotellacalledealcala.com | Budget)*, a mid-class hotel surrounded by greenery with comfortable rooms, air conditioning, a restaurant, bar and pool.

MONTEZUMA (126 B3) (*D6*)

Start the day by saluting the sun and enjoy the evening under a fabulous starry sky with a cocktail in the beach bar – live and let live is the motto in the fishing village of Montezuma (pop. 1,000) in the outer south, where lots of escapists and ageing hippies join the *ticos*. The lovely, unspoilt sandy beach is surrounded by cliffs, the jungle reaches almost as far as the water, and the cafés, small restaurants and hotels, some really quite improvised, are trendy meeting places. There is even a *Farmer's Market*

Beaches, as far as the eye can see: Nicoya Peninsula

Stalactites in the 62-m/203.4-ft deep Terciopelo cave in the Barra Honda National Park

(Sat 9am–1pm | Parque Principal) with organically grown fruit and vegetables and wholefood cakes.

NICOYA (122 C5) (*m C4*)

This small town (pop. 28,000) in the middle of the peninsula is the cultural centre, and a perfect stop-off on the way to the coast. Based on the foundation walls of an old Chorotega settlement by the Spanish in 1544, it has the country's second-oldest church. The *Iglesia de San Blas* (after the town's old name) was built in 1634 on the place where the vanquished *indígenas* had their cult site. The place of worship, white with red tiles and an impressive bell tower, is opposite the mango tree-shaded *Parque Central*. If you wish to stay overnight, go to the *Hotel Curime (20 rooms | Ctra. 150 | Curime | 2 km/1.2 mi south of the town on the road to Sáma-ra | tel. 26 85 52 38 | Budget)* opposite the bus stop to Liberia (large rooms with bathrooms).

PARQUE NACIONAL BARRA HONDA (122 C5) (*m C4*)

Experience for cave visitors and Batman fans: this park, 20 km/12.4 mi northeast of Nicoya and measuring 8.9 mi^2, consists of a vast network of karst caves, 19 researched stalactite caves inhabited by colonies of bats, and many other caves that have not yet been researched. Streams flow through the caves, sometimes waterfalls from one cave to the next. At the moment, only two caves are open to visitors.

To visit the caves, you must have the required equipment, experience and support. The park management offers tours, but you must book in advance. It is also worth walking along the signposted *Sendero Ceiba* to ☀ a *lookout point* with views over the tropical forest and the Nicoya Peninsula. *Park daily 8am–4pm | US$12, visit to the Terciopelo cave US$30 (admission to the park included) | tel. 26 59 15 51 | www.nicoyapeninsula. com/barrahonda*

PARQUE NACIONAL PALO VERDE
(122–123 C–D4) *(ⓜ C3–4)*

Meeting place for ornithologists: 23.2 mi² of marshland (30 km/18.6 mi south-west of Las Cañas) offering protection for lots of species of waterfowl *(Laguna Foohas)* and migratory birds. There are also crocodiles in the river. *Daily 8am–4pm | US$10*

The INSIDER **TIP** *Station Palo Verde (double rooms US$180 all-inclusive | www.ots.ac.cr)* of the OTS (Organisation for Tropical Studies) offers accommodation in rustic lodges with bathroom and fan, vegetarian meals and a guided tour of the nature park – ideal for animal-lovers.

SÁMARA (122 B6) *(ⓜ B5)*

40 km/24.9 mi south of Nicoya on the west of the peninsula is the palm-studded *Playa Sámara*, which can also be accessed on a domestic flight (airport 4 km/2.5 mi to the east). The gently rounded bay, bordered by the Punto Indio cliff, has one of the safest and quietest beaches in Costa Rica. It is very busy, especially at the weekends, because wealthy *ticos* have their summer homes in Sámara.

On the Playa Buena Vista, 6 km/3.7 mi west of Sámara, in the middle of a large garden and 250 m/820 ft from the beach, is the *Flying Crocodile (10 rooms | tel. 26 56 80 48 | www.flying-crocodile. com | Budget–Moderate)*. The owners offer sightseeing flights in a microlight *(20 mins from US$110)*.

To the north-west is *Nosara* on an often deserted beach that is occasionally visited by monkeys. The town centre is 3.5 km/2.2 mi from the beach. The destination for those who are interested in spiritualism is INSIDER **TIP** *Pacha Mama (tel. 87 85 89 49 | www.pachamama.com)* 10 km/6.2 mi north of Nosara between Ostional and Juanillo, a non-commercial centre with 100 long-term residents and room for 200 visitors with an interest in yoga and meditation. Accommodation is in a tent, in *casitas* or bungalows.

TAMARINDO (122 A4) *(ⓜ A4)*

Whether surfing, partying or relaxing on a beach, you can do it all – and more – in Playa Tamarindo (pop. 3,500). As one of the hottest spots in the entire region, it also has a selection of the best restaurants, exceptional boutiques and Spanish language schools. By day, the propeller aircraft from San José land at the tiny airport, but there are also plenty of options for finding peaceful bliss. For instance, just north of the Playa Grande. in a garden surrounded by palm trees on the beach is the hotel *Tamarindo Diria (240 rooms. | tel. 26 53 00 32 | www.tamarindodiria.com | Moderate–Expensive)* with an excellent restaurant. There a wonderful views of the ocean and sunset from the ☀ upstairs rooms.

Across the river north of Tamarindo on the Playa Grande is the small, friendly *Hotel Cantarana (5 rooms | tel. 26 53 04 86 | www.hotel-cantarana.com | Moderate)* with a pool and restaurant. Between November and March turtles come onto the beach to lay their eggs.

LOW BUDGET

Playa Tamarindo is the place for an inexpensive beach holiday. There are camp sites, inexpensive B&Bs, cool beach bars and basic restaurants.

The lovely, inexpensive ceramics, some of which have pre-Columbian designs, are made by women in *Guaitil* in old-fashioned kilns.

PACIFIC COAST

Surveying, planning and building is underway on the dark sand beaches of the Pacific Coast, because the proximity to the central high valley – less than a two-hour drive away, and there are hourly buses – makes the coast more appealing to city folk.

Puntarenas and, increasingly, beaches such as Manuel Antonio and Playa de Jacó have long benefited from the boom, and there's plenty going on everywhere at the weekends. The tourism infrastructure on the Pacific Coast is far more developed than on the Caribbean side. However, the Pacific Coast in the south of Costa Rica is isolated and largely unspoilt, and was made wealthy by the banana industry. Following the demise of this monocul-ture, the poor region has now put its trust in eco-tourism.

GOLFITO

(131 E3) (*L10*) **The approximately six-hour drive from San José to Golfito, which takes you all through Costa Rica's different types of landscape, is an experience in itself.**

It starts off with hairpin bends up to the highest pass in the country, the 349-m/1,145-ft Cerro de la Muerte, usually shrouded in mist, and then up in more tight bends to the Valle del General. There are miles and miles of green pineapple fields covering the red earth. In the La Amistad National Park,

Tourism is booming on the beaches of the Pacific Coast: enjoy nature and the ocean between Puntarenas and Golfito

the road follows river courses and passes waterfalls.

The air turns humid and the vegetation becomes tropical at Palmar Norte: there are orchids, bananas, palm trees. Soon you will see Golfito, now the smallest port in the country and stretching 6 km/3.7 mi along a lagoon of the Golfo Dulce. Half a century ago, the port was the no. 1 for the transportation of bananas; 20,000 people settled in the area, and bars and brothels opened in the old town. It's quieter today. A new free-trade zone *(depósito,* tax-free shopping) and the development of tourism is intended to bring in visitors and create jobs.

Pueblo Cívico is the oldest part of Golfito, and is in the south of the town. You'll find hotels, restaurants and bars here as well as a small dock *(muellecito)* for boats and water taxis for rides to the beaches. This quarter has not yet been restored, and you will still see old wooden houses on stilts, partly over the water. The current town centre starts on the northern edge of Pueblo Cívico, such as at the Centro

Turístico Samoa Sur, and further north is the wealthy *Zona Americana*.

SIGHTSEEING

REFUGIO NACIONAL DE VIDA SILVESTRE GOLFITO

Camping is permitted in the 5 mi², freely accessible animal reserve and tropical rainforest just outside the town. The

gets busy at Happy Hour and when there is the regular live music. *Daily | Ctra. 14/ km 3/mi 1.9 | tel. 27 75 01 92 | Moderate*

SAMOA DEL SUR ☆

A large open-air pavilion offers local and international cuisine with ocean views. *At the Samoa del Sur Resort | tel. 27 75 02 33 | www.samoadelsur.com | Moderate*

Not only a delight at sundown: ceviche

best time to visit is between January and March, when it is relatively dry. You will see lots of orchid and bird varieties in the park.

FOOD & DRINK

MAR Y LUNA ☆

Enjoy the sunset, the small harbour and the open ocean from the terrace with a beer in your hand – and afterwards, how about a tomato salad and guacamole? Or perhaps *ceviche* and a *mariscada* (with fish and crustaceans: excellent!). It

SHOPPING

DEPÓSITO LIBRE COMERCIAL

To visit the duty-free trading zone, you need to obtain the (free) *TAC (tarjeta de autorización de compra)* the day before; you'll need your passport for this. All visitors may spend a maximum of US$1,000 (twice a year). Around 50 shops cell clothing, spirits, electronic goods, cosmetics, car accessories and much more. *TAC: Mon 1pm–8pm, Tue–Sat 8am–8pm, shopping Tue–Sat 8am–4.30pm, Sun 7am–3pm | North side of the city near the airport | www.deposi todegolfito.com*

BEACHES

PLAYA CACAO

The dark gravel and sandy beach is surrounded by dense rainforest – pure Robinson feeling – and the transport is right, too: you can cross by water taxi (around US$4) from the dock in Golfito (Muellecito).

ZANCUDO

Zancudo Peninsula is surrounded by isolated beaches. 15 km/9.3 mi south of Golfito is the *Playa Zancudo* with black sand. Staggering under the weight of their cool bags, people board the water taxis at the main harbour of Muellecito in the mornings (around US$6), a terrific half-hour experience: through the mangrove-covered estuary of Esperanza. There are inexpensive restaurants and places to stay, such as *Cabinas Sol y Mar (tel. 27 76 00 14 | www.zancudo.com | Budget)* with well-priced huts by the sea, effectively at the end of the world. To the south is 6-km/3.7-mi long, flat *Zancudo Beach*, perfect for surfing.

ENTERTAINMENT

INSIDER TIP ▶ BAR LA BOMBA

A bomb! The meeting place for adventurers, lonely travellers, individualists and groups since 1946. Old photos on the walls of the restored bar tell Golfito's history. *Daily 11am–midnight | Ctra. 14/ Pueblo Civil | Next to the service station | tel. 27 75 21 49 | www.bomba-golfito.com*

WHERE TO STAY

BUENA VISTA CABINAS ꙮ

Peter, the owner, receives his guests in his lodge. Lovely: the location adjoining a 54-acre rainforest and the views of Golfo Dulce. There is also a small pool! *4 rooms | Ctra. Golfito–Purruja, km 6/ mi 3.7 | tel. 27 75 20 65 | petergolfito@ hotmail.com | Budget*

EL GRAN CEIBO

Hotel (four buildings) at the southern end of Golfito by the sea with two pools, a subtropical garden and ꙮ breakfast in the open air with ocean views. There are rooms with and without air conditioning and noise. *27 rooms | Av. Principal | tel. 27 75 04 03 | Budget*

LA PURRUJA LODGE

Various cabins on a small hill; Swiss management. Trips to the Osa Peninsula; river, jungle, cave, crocodile and riding tours. There is also a pleasant camp site. *5 rooms | 5 km/3.1 mi south of Golfito | tel. 27 75 50 54 | www.purruja.com | Budget*

SIERRA

Mid-class establishment surrounded by greenery, north of the town. Large

★ **Parque Nacional Corcovado**
The "Amazon of Costa Rica"
→ p. 68

★ **Bahía Drake**
Clean beaches in a natural
paradise → p. 68

★ **Parque Nacional Manuel Antonio**
Swim in the country's loveliest
bays → p. 75

★ **La Mariposa**
Hotel breakfast overlooking the
Manuel Antonio National Park
→ p. 76

MARCO POLO HIGHLIGHTS

rooms, two pools, the specialities restaurant *Aramacao* and a large selection of tours. Personal choice: the hotel casino and karaoke bar. *72 rooms | Ctra. Principal Norte between depósito and the airport | Zona Americana | tel. 22 75 06 66 | www.hotelsierra.com | Moderate*

INFORMATION

ICT TOURIST OFFICE
Inter-American Highway | Río Claro (19 km/11.8 mi north of Golfito), 100 m/328 ft east of the service station | tel. 27 89 77 39 |

WHERE TO GO

PARQUE INTERNACIONAL LA AMISTAD
(128–129 C–E 4–5) (*M K–M 6–8*)
Costa Rica's biggest nature reserve (734 mi² on Costa Rican territory) crosses the border to Panama; it is also the least visited. Wilderness, few roads and trails, that you will travel in the company of a local guide. The biodiversity – deciduous and pine forests, tropical rainforest and moors, wasteland covered in low shrubs and grasses – surpasses all other national parks. There are 400 species of bird here, along with over 250 amphibians and reptiles plus tapir, jaguar, puma, ocelot, mountain lion and several types of monkey. It's very difficult to enter on your own; cul-de-sacs from the

CA 2, the southern Interamericana, end on the outskirts of the reserve. Independent travel agencies offer expeditions.

PENÍNSULA DE OSA (OSA PENINSULA) (130–131 C–D4) (*M J–K10*)
At the beginning of the 1960s, a "wood rush" began on the little-inhabited peninsula, to which by 1975 a significant quantity of precious wood had fallen victim – until the ★ *Parque Nacional Corcovado* was established. It covers an area of 162 mi² in the south-west, and contains lots of rare trees, 100 species of reptile, 300 of bird and 150 of mammal. Later on, gold was found in the rivers. Adventurers arrived, seeking their fortune, and there was a regular gold rush – with the result that the destruction of the nature reserve progressed rapidly: there was deforestation, the ground was dug up, rivers diverted. Today, digging in the national park, which is called "our Amazon" in Costa Rica, is banned.

The peninsula is a huge greenhouse, accessible by land, by ferry *(to Puerto Jiménez, 90 min.)* or by charter aircraft. On the north-west side is the ★ *Bahía Drake,* a largely undeveloped natural paradise with a clean beach and dense vegetation growing down to it. Simple, comfortable accommodation is available, and you can fish and go horseback riding. Boat trips to the *Corcovado National Park* and the *Caño Island* bio reserve

BEEF TO BURGERS

They are made from beef, and every year Costa Rica supplies 100,000 tonnes of that for fast-food chains. There are now more cattle than people in the country, and grazing areas have

been extended at the cost of the forests. After all, each head of cattle needs several acres of pasture before it can be slaughtered. Profits are short-term, the damage to the country long-lasting.

The dense greenery provides a home for numerous animals: Corcovado National Park

arrange all the accommodation in the bay. Basic, rustic accommodation in *Agujitas* is available in Bahía Drake 350 m/ 1,148 ft from the beach at *Cabinas Manolo (10 rooms | tel. 2775 09 29 | www.ca binasmanolo.com | Budget)*; also inexpensive excursions and tours. Arrival in Drake Bay: in Sierpe take a boat that travels down the Río Sierpe into the bay *(40 km/24.9 mi | 80 min US$20–30)*.

JACÓ

(127 D3) (ψ F6) **A large, rounded bay with a dark lava beach, luscious green coconut palms and a strong surf that is popular with surfers: the Pacific town of Jacó, for decades the meeting place for young backpackers, has become a mid-class bathing resort for the *ticos*.**
As well as lots of *cabañas* and small guesthouses at medium prices, all-inclusive resorts and luxury hotels, apart- ments and holiday homes are under construction. Jacó is currently the fastest growing town in the country, and has more discotheques and clubs than anywhere else in Costa Rica. What some people like puts others off: the tourist bustle in Jacó (pop. 11,000), 65 km/40.4 mi north-west of Quepos, has grown considerably, but sadly has also brought with it the downside (drugs, prostitution and petty crime). None the less, the relaxed atmosphere and (for Costa Rica) large number of restaurants, bars and shops may well encourage you to stay for a few more days and see more of the surrounding area.

SIGHTSEEING

PARQUE NACIONAL CARARA
Limited in the north by the Río Tárcoles, and situated to the north of Jacó, this 18-mi^2 national park contains a tremendous biodiversity thanks to its

various vegetation zones. It is for example home to one of the largest macaw colonies in the country, the now rare scarlet macaw. These parrots are over 80 cm/31 in long, and announce their presence with a penetrating call. They have a red head, chest and wing tips, and blue and yellow wings. They leave the park at sunrise and sunset to fly to the mangroves on the coast. You're most likely to see the birds with a local guide, for instance from *Vic Tours (2 hours without park admission US$35 | tel. 26 45 10 15 | www.victourscostarica.com)*. There are two trails on the west side of the park, one of which runs 500 m/1,640 ft south of the bridge over the Río Tárcoles, where you will usually see crocodiles on the river bank. *Daily 8am–4pm | US$10*

Even though this might look like an afternoon nap, keep your distance!

FOOD & DRINK

ANFITEATRO ●

The terraces with tables go down the mountain like in a Greek theatre, and the huge trees are home to parrots, toucans and monkeys. The views of the Pacific and the landscape are spectacular, the menu excellent, from the penne with frutti di mare to the grilled tuna or lamb. Regular concerts bathe the tropical scenery in classical music and jazz. *Hotel Villa Caletas | Herradura, 2 km/1.2 mi west N34, 6 km/3.7 mi north of Jacó | tel. 26 30 30 00 | www.hotelvillacaletas.com |* Expensive

INSIDER TIP GRAFFITI RESTRO CAFÉ & WINE BAR

The ingredients are right at the "Cheddar Burger", which makes fast food (almost) a pleasure. There are a few dishes on the daily menu that will fill you up, while dessert has to be a strong coffee à la maison. At the back of a shopping centre. *Mon–Sat from 5pm | Pacific Center 23/Av. Pastor Díaz | tel. 26 43 17 08 |* Moderate

LEMON ZEST

The restaurant on the top floor of a shopping centre has many fans – mainly because the dishes are made using ingredients from local suppliers and are always freshly prepared. *Daily from 5pm | El Jardín Plaza/Av. Pastor Díaz/C/ Hicaco | 1st floor | tel. 26 43 25 91 | www.lemonzest jaco.com | Moderate*

SHOPPING

THE COSTA RICA COFFEE EXPERIENCE
Whether "Organic Vanilla" or "Cinnamon", fresh, delicious (you can try before you buy) and inexpensive coffee, plus cake and chocolate, unusual T-shirts. ceramics from Nicaragua and original crafts from ⊙ rainforest projects and environmental initiatives. *Av. Pastor Díaz | Opposite Banco Nacional*

LEISURE & SPORTS

AERIAL TRAM ☀
Another *Rainforest Aerial Tramway* opened north of Jacó with a gondola through the jungle. A one-hour ride – also with sea views – goes up and beyond the treetops, past a 15-m/49.2-ft waterfall and into the middle of the rainforest. The 222-acre site also has a zip line and a snake enclosure *(serpentarium). Daily 7am–4pm | US$65 | 3 km/1.9 mi north of Jacó | www.rain forestadventure.com*

BEACHES

The 4-km/2.5-mi long *Playa de Jacó* runs between the town and the sea, flanked by numerous beach cafés and restaurants. The sea is rough, and you must take care when swimming. The further south you go, the quieter it gets. At the Playa Herradura, 6 km/3.7 mi to the north, you'll also find dark sand, but it's quieter here and safer to swim.

WHERE TO STAY

We strongly advise against the very cheap options in Jacó. Time and again, visitors tell of thefts and unclean, unsafe rooms. Despite the increase in popularity, prices remain moderate so you really would do well to choose a mid-priced hotel.

LOS SUEÑOS MARRIOTT
The resort which thrones, park-like, between the Pacific and the rainforest, was built in the lavish Spanish colonial style, and is one of the few major luxury hotels in Costa Rica. Flawless pool landscapes, six elegantly designed restaurants, rooms and suites with views of the Bay of Herradura, plus a casino, golf and tennis courts, and various fitness and wellness offers. Shuttle to Jacó. *200 rooms | Playa Herradura, 800 m/2,625 ft west*

LOW BUDGET

The Tucan (150 m/492 ft east of the Pacific Road | tel. 27 43 81 40 | www.tucanhotel.com) in Uvita has good value air conditioned multiple-bed and double rooms. As well as a bar and restaurant, it has a communal kitchen, free Internet, and surfboard, bicycle and motorbike hire.

● *Outdoor Movie Nights* are held in the new harbour for sports boats in Quepos, Pez Vela marina. Classic films are shown at about 7pm on Fridays from January to March. Visitors make themselves comfortable on the ground on or large cushions bean bags in the little open-air cinema in the harbour. Admission free!

of Herradura | tel. 26 30 90 00 | www.
marriott.com | *Expensive*

Relaxing beach:
Playa de Jacó

MAR DE LUZ ✪
This family-friendly eco hotel is 200 m/
656 ft from the beach, and is solar
powered. There are colourful, rustic
(some with stone walls) rooms, a small

library in the open lounge area, a pool
and well-tended garden, and even a
children's play area and a playroom
– all for a very good price. Need we
suggest you book well in advance? *29
rooms | Av. Pastor Díaz | Next to Sub-
way | tel. 26 43 30 00 | www.mardeluz.
com | Moderate*

VILLA CALETAS ☆☆
Style, romance and tropical nature combined with breathtaking views of the
Nicoya Peninsula at the resort hotel up
on a mountain. The French colonial-style
resort is still one of the loveliest (and
most expensive) in the country. Even the
standard rooms are luxurious hideaways.
The Junior suites are bigger and have
their own plunge pools with views of the
Pacific bay far below. Transport service to
the private beach on the Playa Herradura and two wonderful restaurants. *Herra-
dura | 2 km/1.2 mi west N34, 6 km/3.7 mi
north of Jacó | tel. 26 30 30 00 | www.
hotelvillacaletas.com | Expensive*

INFORMATION

There is no ICT Office; information is available from the information desk of the
Rainforest Aerial Tramway (see p. 71).

PUNTARENAS

**(126 C2) (∅ E5) Traditional bathing re-
sort for *ticos*, capital (pop. 100,000)
of the province of the same name, the
country's main Pacific harbour until the
development of Puerto Caldera in the
south.**

Puntarenas, which grew from coffee
trade, covers a 6-km/3.7-mi headland
in the Gulf of Nicoya, and seals off the
lagoon and El Estero Bay in the south.
The humid subtropical climate is ideal

for growing the rice, bananas and coconut palms for which Puntarenas is still a trading centre.

On the south side of the city is a long stretch of beach where the locals have their second homes – this is where the boats are. And yet, the days of prosperity are over, because Caldera port is now where it's at. Entire blocks of houses are showing signs of decline, but there are hopes that the burgeoning tourism industry will help to create new jobs.

SIGHTSEEING

Because of the heat and humidity, it's best to walk around the peninsula, which is about 50 Calles long and only four or five Avenidas wide, in the morning or after 4pm. A stroll along the beach promenade *Paseo de los Turistas* (south side) will take you past pleasant restaurants, cafés and bars; to the north of the city, you'll pass the harbour basin with docks, warehouses and ferry terminals – the working world of a port. The streets of the city centre *(Calles 1–7)* and the *market (Mercado Municipal) (Av. 3/C/ 2)* bustle with life in the mornings.

MUSEO HISTÓRICO DE LA CIUDAD DE PUNTARENAS
There are little exhibitions telling the history of the city, its port and coffee. The black-and-white pictures taken at the last turn of the century are interesting. *Mon–Sat 9am–noon, 1pm–5pm | admission free | Av. Central/C/ 1 | Casa de la Cultura*

INSIDER TIP PARQUE MARINO DEL PACÍFICO ●
The attractions include the crocodile breeding basins, the turtles and tropical fish in the beautifully designed state park that is committed to protecting the ocean. *Tue–Sun 9am–4.30pm | US$10 | Av. 4 | Old station, 500 m/1,640 ft east of the cruise ship pier | www.parquemarino.org*

PLAZA CENTRAL
The role of the Parque Central is here played by a small plaza with a 100-year-old, massive sandstone church. A pedestrian area starts at the north-east end of the square *(C/ 5–7)*.

FOOD & DRINK

CAPITÁN MORENO
Juicy steaks, generous plates of seafood and a large selection of craft beers. And parties: DJs, bands, dancing and general merry-making. *Paseo de los Turistas/C/ 13–15 | tel. 26 61 08 10 | Moderate*

LA CASA DE LOS MARISCOS
The restaurant is particularly popular with ticos, and offers fish dishes with sea views, exotic mixed drinks and home-made desserts. *C/ 5/Av. 4 | tel. 26 61 16 66 | Moderate*

SHOPPING

Sugar-sweet mangos, mini bananas by the dozen and *pan dulce* (sweet bread) are well-priced at the *Mercado Municipal (Av. 3/C/ 2)*.

LEISURE & SPORTS

Todo incluido is the deal on the all-day *Tortuga Island Cruise*. A catamaran goes to uninhabited Tortuga Island for snorkelling in the crystal-clear water, white beaches, nature and buffets on the sandy beach. Organised by *Calypso Tours (from US$145 | tel. 22 56 27 27 | www.calypsocruises.com)*.

BEACH

On the south side of the town is a 5-km/3.1-mi long beach with infrastructure. As there are also lots of hotels and the cruise ship pier with 100 ships a year, there's always plenty going on – especially at weekends.

ENTERTAINMENT

It's best to visit one of the bars or restaurants on the Paseo de los Turistas; it's not so hot any more, and watching the sun set over the mountains of Nicoya is a sight you'll never forget.

WHERE TO STAY

INSIDER TIP HOTEL VISTA GOLFO

Above the town in the mountains, with horse riding, canopy and jungle tours. *11 rooms | Finca Daniel | Miramar de Montes de Oro | Tajo Alto | tel. 26 39 83 03 | www. finca-daniel.com | Moderate*

TIOGA

Somewhat faded elegance with a casino, garden and pool. ꖸ Restaurant with sea views, inexpensive *sodas* by the pool. *52 rooms | C/ 19/Av. 4 | tel. 26 61 02 71 | www.hoteltioga.com | Moderate*

YADRÁN

Modern establishment opposite a sheltered beach (with a road between). ꖸ panorama restaurant, children's pool. *36 rooms | Paseo de los Turistas/C/ 35 (El Carmen) | tel. 26 61 26 62 | www. hotelyadrancr.com | Moderate–Expensive*

INFORMATION

ICT TOURIST OFFICE

Plaza del Pacífico | Paseo de los Turistas/C/ Central | tel. 26 61 64 08 | www.puntarenas.com

QUEPOS

(127 F4) *(𝄐 G7)* **Beaches, lodges and rainforest: Quepos (pop. 12,000) is the entrance to Manuel Antonio, Costa Rica's best-known national park, a few miles away. The former banana port has retained its typical flair.**

Puerto Quepos was built as an export harbour, but after the banana plantations were destroyed by an epidemic in the 1950s, things started to go downhill. As you approach, you'll notice the little town's pretty location among hilly forests. That may have been what caused the Franciscans to build a mission station on Naranjo River in 1570, although they abandoned it in 1730. Only a few foundation walls are left of the station. Today Quepos consists of Boca Vieja, an old village of pile dwellings near the bridge over the funnel-shaped estuary, the bungalows of the former banana growers outside the town, and the relatively new centre.

Theft and cons are the order of the day on the road from Quepos to the Manuel Antonio National Park, and in Manuel Antonio in particular. Con artists, sometimes even wearing uniforms, use whistles in a threatening manner, pretending to be the police and stopping and menacing drivers (car parks, tour and hotel organisers, shopping). INSIDER TIP Just keep driving.

SIGHTSEEING

ISLA DAMAS

The elongated peninsula near Quepos forms a lagoon into which four rivers flow. There are dense mangroves around the river mouth, the estuary, which is also home to lots of water fowl. *Boat trips from Quepos Marina | From US$50*

PARQUE NACIONAL MANUEL ANTONIO ★ ●

The village outside the park is a large flea market with goods from the Far East and Central America, and pushy sellers. The national park is well visited all year round. be back at the starting point in an hour. None the less, the biodiversity here is no less than anywhere else that guarantees contact with monkeys. *Tue–Sun 7am–4pm | US$16 | 7 km/4.4 mi south-east of the town | www.manuelantoniopark.com*

Tree residents in the Manuel Antonio National Park: capuchin monkeys

The three bays of the almost 2.7 mi² national park are considered the loveliest in the country; two of them, the white beach bays *Espadilla Sur* and *Manuel Antonio,* are separated by the impressive rock formation *Punta Catedral*. Lots of lizards, water fowl, raccoons and monkeys, and 200 bird species. The park also has 12 small islands that you can see from the shore: breeding ground for sea birds.

Useful for visitors with children who can't walk very far yet but still want to see the monkeys: INSIDER TIP the park has several circular trails, and if you like you can

FOOD & DRINK

INSIDER TIP BROOKLYN BAKERY

This small, typical Caribbean wooden house smells of freshly roasted coffee and chocolate cake. A dream: the tropical milk shakes! *Mon–Sat 8am–6pm | Av. 1 | tel. 27 77 77 02 | Budget*

EL PATIO DE CAFÉ MILAGRO

Cult meeting place for young Americans: this coffee roastery, which was established by a college student, offers coffee specialities, while the colourful open-air restaurant serves Costa Rican specialities and international cuisine, including fish, from breakfast until dinner as well as cocktails and South American wines. Happy Hour in the neighbouring *Bistro Latino* is daily from 4pm-6pm, with live music Mon–Sat from 7pm–9pm. *Daily 7am–11pm | Ctra. Quepos a Manuel Antonio | tel. 27 77 07 94 | www.cafemilagro. com | Moderate*

RUNAWAY GRILL RESTAURANT & FISH BAR
Happy Hour and sunsets and a "you hook them, we cook them" offer for anglers. Dinner followed by a visit to the *Outdoor Movie Nights* (see p. 71) is an excellent combination. *Daily from 11.30am | Marina Pez Vela/Paseo del Mar | At the new harbour for sports boats | tel. 25 19 90 95 | www.runaway grill.com | Moderate–Expensive*

(see p. 71)

SHOPPING

JAIME PELIGRO BOOKS & ADVENTURES
Large selection of books, new and used, and lots of coffee-table books of Costa Rica and travel guides, plus tourist information and tour organiser. *Av. Central/C/ 2 (opposite El Pueblo restaurant) | www. queposbooks.com*

LEISURE & SPORTS

Amigos del Río (Ctra. a Manuel Antonio / km 2/mi 1.2 | tel. 27 77 00 82 | www.ami gosdelrio.net) offers boat trips out onto the ocean as well as white-water rafting, horse riding and jungle hikes.

BEACHES
The Manuel Antonio National Park also has the easily accessible dream beaches *Espadilla Sur* and *Playa Manuel Antonio*.

The vegetation, which reaches almost down to the water, and the little monkeys on the look-out for anything edible create a tropical atmosphere. The *Playa Espadilla Norte* lies to the north. Then come the many miles of INSIDER TIP *Playa Escondida*, as far as the Punta Quepos Peninsula. It's a lot quieter here, and almost deserted at weekends.

WHERE TO STAY

Opt for the lodges on the road to Manuel Antonio Park: they are quiet and have far-reaching views of the ocean.

ARENAS DEL MAR
Couples aren't the only ones who appreciate having their own jacuzzi on their balcony and access to the private beach bay (with a comfortable recliner): the site goes down to the water, and is perfect for observing animals. *38 rooms | Playa Playitas/ca. 1.5 km/0.9 mi south of the National Park | tel. 27 77 27 77 | www. arenasdelmar.com | Expensive*

GAIA ● ◉
Elegant, understated design that harmonises perfectly with the surrounding lavish nature, and perfects the experience of peace. The luxurious hotel has rooms and suites with a pleasant atmosphere, terraces with chic rattan furniture and a pleasant spa. Just as pleasing: the owners are committed to social responsibility: they support the village community, help to prevent drug abuse, support clinics and nursery schools, and much more. *20 rooms | Ctra. Quepos a Manuel Antonio, km 2.7/mi 1.7 | tel. 27 77 97 97 | www. gaiahr.com | Expensive*

LA MARIPOSA ★ ☆
One of the prettiest establishments in the country, suites in bungalows high above

Swimming in the national park: Playa Espadilla in the Parque Nacional Manuel Antonio

the sea, furnished with antiques and ethnic objects, lookout platform over the bay. The furniture on the restaurant terrace glows in pink and turquoise. *56 rooms and suites | 4 km/2.5 mi south of Quepos on the road to Manuel Antonio | tel. 27 77 03 55 | www.hotelmariposa.com | Expensive*

VILLA ROMANTICA ●
Surrounded by nature: a stairway leads to the veranda off the rooms (air conditioning or fan). Tropical garden and pool. *16 rooms | km 0.5 on the road to Manuel Antonio | tel. 27 77 00 37 | www.villa romantica.com | Moderate*

WIDE MOUTH FROG
Hotel in a large tropical garden. As well as five dormitories for up to 42 guests, there are also 12 comfortable two- and three-bed rooms. People meet up with other travellers by the pool and in the kitchen or relax in the hammocks. *Av. Central/C/ 1 | 150 m/492 ft east of the bus stop | tel. 27 77 27 98 | www.widemouth frog.org | Budget*

ICT TOURIST OFFICE
Edifício del PIMA | Camino al Muelle | tel. 27 77 42 17

WHERE TO GO

INSIDER TIP **RESORT & SPA CRISTAL BALLENA** (128 B6) (*ᗰ J8*)
7 km/4.4 mi south of Uvita, a good 70 km/43.5 mi from Quepos, situated on a hill of the Costa Ballena in the Parque Nacional Marino Ballena is the Resort & Spa Cristal Ballena. This luxurious, Austrian-run Mediterranean-style hotel with a large pool situated in the middle of a tropical park has spacious ⚘ rooms with balconies from which you can see the marine national park. As well as boat tours and whale watching, the activities also include game fishing, snorkelling and canopy. *19 rooms | Ctra. Costera Sur, km 169/ mi 105 | tel. 27 86 53 54 | www.cristal-ballena.com | Expensive*

CARIBBEAN COAST

Brightly-coloured wooden houses on stilts, deserted beaches with pelicans and frigate birds, fishing canoes under the palm trees, the smell of the ocean and coconut in the air. Tourists might be greeted with "Hey, man" when they visit the tiny settlements on the humid Caribbean coast – an invitation to further discourse.

While 98% of the population in the rest of Costa Rica is light-skinned, one-third of the population in the province of Limón is black, descendants of the people who were brought from the West Indies to work in the plantations and build the railway. Many of them speak the English dialect that is widespread in Jamaica. Not only is the language different here, but so too is the lifestyle – music, cuisine and the way of life are undeniably Caribbean. The province is not widely inhabited: there are only 300,000 people on the 200-km/124-mi long Atlantic coast.

PUERTO LIMÓN

(129 E2) (*M L5*) **One of the main harbours in the country is Puerto Limón (pop. 80,000), container port for coffee, pineapples and bananas, and the centre of Afro-Caribbean culture.**
The area is starting to look slightly shabby; there is a noticeable increase in corrugated metal, paint is flaking, and much of the damage from earthquakes has still

Caribbean lifestyle on the Atlantic coast, reggae music in the beach bars, tropical vegetation on the canals of Tortuguero

not been removed; there are ruins by the sea. Because of the hot, humid climate (no dry season), the tourists are mostly day visitors stopping off on their way to the Tortuguero canals and the Caribbean beaches in the south.

SIGHTSEEING

CORREO

The large corner house, built at the turn of the century before last, has the love-liest windows, balconies and doors in town, and is painted in pretty pastel shades. *South side of the Mercado Municipal*

MUSEO ETNOHISTÓRICO

Masks, drums and puppets – the wide-spread voodoo cult of the Caribbean is concealed by the Afro-Caribbeans of Costa Rica. So much better, then, that answers to any initial questions about it are available in the tiny museum on the first floor of the old post office. Impressive: the exhibition of the construction

Helpers at the plantation in Bribrí packing bananas for export

of the railway to Limón. *Tue–Sat 9am–noon and 1pm–4pm | US$2 | Av. 2/C/ 4 | South side of the Mercado in the old post office | First floor*

rice, chicken dishes, baked bananas, fish etc.) in a large, spotlessly clean restaurant. *C/ 6/Av. 3–4 | tel. 27 58 32 49 | Moderate*

FOOD & DRINK

Several *sodas* and Chinese restaurants, also serving Creole cuisine, on the *Mercado Municipal (Av. 2–3/C/ 3–4)*. Best choice for fish and seafood: the cooking spots in the middle of the market. Great atmosphere and lots of reggae music in the cafés and restaurants on the *Playa Bonita*.

BRISAS DEL CARIBE
Outdoor tables and views of the Parque Vargas opposite. Serves Caribbean dishes, and "international" ones for more cautious tourists. *Av. 2/C/ 1 | tel. 27 58 01 38 | Moderate*

KALISI COFFEE SHOP
The place to go to meet locals. Down-to-earth Caribbean cuisine (coconut

SHOPPING

The town's shopping district is near the *Cruise Ship Pier (Av. 1)* and on the road from there to the centre. It has the usual souvenirs, but also wood carvings and little boxes made of hardwood with tiny drawers, and ceramic figures. The Mercado Central offers food, souvenirs and craft items.

LEISURE & SPORTS

Bird-watching, horse-riding, tree-climbing and canopy are on offer at the *Selva Bananito Lodge (Bananito) (tel. 22 53 81 18 | www.selvabananito. com | Where: turn 1 km/0.6 mi south of the bridge over the Río Vizcaya, then 12 km/7.5 mi inland). 20 km/12.4 mi south of Limón*

BRISAS DE LA JUNGLA

Eco adventure park: whizz through the rainforest on a zip line, or find deep relaxation on a walk along the jungle trail with a guide and see the trees where the sloths sleep, sniff the heliconia and then enjoy a pineapple and cocoa smoothies in the bamboo restaurant. *Fri–Sun 10am–9pm | admission US$20 (zip line tour US$50) | Río Blanca, Ctr. 32/towards San José | tel. 88 54 83 01 | www.brisas delajungla.com*

BEACH

The local beach is the golden *Playa Bonita*, 5 km/3.1 mi to the north-west on the road to Moín. The waves also attract surfers, other sports are also offered, and there are several bars and cafés.

ENTERTAINMENT

We advise against heading to Puerto Limón's bars on your own and after dark. It's better to take a taxi to bars in the evenings!

WHERE TO STAY

Avoid cheap accommodation in Limón – the clientele there tends to consist of the sort of people you would avoid at home.

MATAMA

Quiet and in an almost tropical location, large hotel near the beach (350 m/ 1,148 ft, road between) 3 km/1.9 mi north-west of the town. Large garden with a mini zoo. Also trips to Tortuguero and Cahuita. *16 rooms | Playa Bonita | Ctra. a Portete | tel. 27 58 11 23 | Moderate*

PARK HOTEL

Old wooden building that is now a modern mid-class hotel; ☀☀ (balcony) rooms with a safe and sea views, the restaurant serves regional and international cuisine. *32 rooms | Av. 3/C/ 1–2 | tel. 27 98 05 55 | www.parkhotellimon.com | Moderate*

PLAYA WESTFALIA

Best choice: almost luxurious hacienda-style beach hotel in a garden with palm trees, a pool and a beach restaurant. ☀☀ Lovely balcony or terrace rooms with sea views. *8 rooms | Ctra. a Cahuita | 1.5 km/0.9 mi south of the air strip | tel. 47 02 18 85 | www.hotelplayawest falia.com | Moderate–Expensive*

INFORMATION

There is no ICT office in Limón; if necessary go to the *Museum* (see p. 79).

WHERE TO GO

BRIBRÍ (129 E3) (*M6*)

The town is home to Talamanca Indians who work hard at harvest time for little remuneration, and a destination for travellers who are interested in the culture of the *indígenas*. The village with basic wooden houses surrounded by banana

MARCO POLO HIGHLIGHTS

★ **Tortuguero**
A boat ride through the jungle, perfect for watching the animals → p. 84

★ **Turtle Beach**
At Tortuguero National Park, visitors can (carefully) watch the turtles laying their eggs → p. 85

★ **Barra del Colorado**
Living in jungle hotels amidst the maze of lagoons and canals → p. 87

plantations lies 60 km/37.3 mi south of Puerto Limón on the border to Panama, and with its surrounding area makes up an Indian reservation. The meeting place is the turquoise *Restaurante Bribrí (tel. 27510044 | Budget)*.

CAHUITA (129 E3) *(⏷ M6)*

A palm-fringed road, beach to the left, banana plantations to the right, plus

ings. You'd do better to find a hotel or *cabina* on the *Playa Negra* in the north. The *Cahuita National Park (daily 8am–5pm | Donations appreciated)* – one of the loveliest national parks in Costa Rica with swamp and mangrove forest, toucans, hummingbirds and ara parrots, monkeys, raccoons and sloths, as well as wonderful white beaches – reaches from Cahuita across the north-east pen-

Music and relaxed chilling: Cahuita

red achiote trees whose fruits the pre-Columbian population used as a dye, runs 43 km/26.7 mi south from Limón to the village of Cahuita, the meeting place for young people who lead a relaxed life on the beach and appreciate the exotically flavoured food in the *sodas* and the cheap beds in the small hotels. Music and conviviality are the order of the day. The centre of the town with the north entrance to the national park has basic hotels, *cabinas* and restaurants but is not particularly attractive; you also have to keep a close eye on your belong-

insula at Puerto Vargas and south along the beach to Punta Caliente. The well-prepared main trail leads through the forest, parallel to the coast and beach. There is a ● free entrance to the national park from Kelly Creek. A *coral reef* is home to almost three dozen types of coral and over 100 different tropical fish. Hotels: The INSIDER TIP ▶ *Casa de las Flores (10 rooms | 200 m/656 ft north of the park entrance | tel. 27550326 | www. lacasadelasfloreshotel.com | Moderate)* offers comfort and a pool close to the park. Highly recommended: the *El En-*

canto Inn (6 rooms. | C/ Playa Negra/C/ Unión | 600 m/1,968 ft from the centre | tel. 27 55 01 13 | elencantocahuita.com | Moderate), a small B&B with American owners. Siatami Lodge (10 cabinas | Cahuita | tel. 75 50 03 74 | Moderate) consists of basic wooden houses in the Caribbean style with terraces and surrounded by 10,764 ft² of garden, 300 m/984 ft from the village.

MANZANILLO (129 F3) (*∅ N6*)

Fans of an unspoilt Afro-Caribbean atmosphere should visit this settlement 75 km/46.6 mi south of Limón: deserted, palm-fringed beaches, fishing boats, and reggae music resounding from cafés and the colourful wooden houses. There's not much to do here apart from chill on the beach, explore the area and enjoy a beer in the evenings at Maxi's, the local bar. At the point where the road ends by a river in the Gandoca Manzanillo nature reserve is where you will find the unusual hotel INSIDER TIP Almendros & Corales (tel. 27 59 90 56 | www.almondsandcorals.com | Expensive), a comfortable place to stay (with full board). The 24 bungalows have fans and bathrooms, wooden jetties between them , and there is a whirlpool under the treetops.

PUERTO VIEJO DE TALAMANCA (129 F3) (*∅ M6*)

The good vibes are in the air: this colourful, lively resort with numerous hotels, restaurants and bars, plus a dark beach, 15 km/9.3 mi south of Cahuita, is a meeting place for young travellers. The hot days are spent playing beach volleyball, and there's surfing between December and April. Don't forget your insect spray, and watch out for the current in the sea! The ⚫ Asociación Talamanqueña de Ecoturismo y Conservación

(C/ Principal | Puerto Viejo de Talamanca | tel. 27 50 01 91 | www.ateccr.org), an organisation for eco-tourism and nature conservation offers fabulous INSIDER TIP trekking and river tours to the indigenous peoples in the jungle.

Inexpensive accommodation in the town and on the beaches to the north and south with cabinas and small hotels scattered over 5 km/3.1 mi. Austrian owners welcome their guests at the Coco Loco Lodge (tel. 27 50 02 81 | www.cocolocolodge.com | Budget), five rustic palm-roofed huts with bathroom and terrace (plus four other rooms), close to the beach and surrounded by a large garden. The INSIDER TIP Hotel Maritza (10 rooms and 14 cabinas | tel. 27 50 00 03 | hotelmaritzapuertoviejolimon.blogspot.com | Moderate) in the centre is a gem, a Caribbean wooden building with plenty of atmosphere.

LOW BUDGET

At the Sloth Sanctuary (Tue–Sun 8am–2pm | Penhurst, 10 km/6.2 mi north of Cahuita | 27 50 07 75 | www.slothsanctuary.com), the world's only sanctuary for sloths, orphaned youngsters are bottled fed until independent. A visit and the terrific tour are an experience, and very well priced (US$30). Interns who help and receive free accommodation in return are (usually) welcome.

At the tiny guesthouse Los Sueños (6 rooms | tel. 27 50 03 69 | www.hotellossuenos.com) in Puerto Viejo de Talamanca, two people can stay in a double room just a block from the beach – for US$30.

The hotel *Le Caméléon (23 rooms | Playa Cocles | tel. 27 50 05 01 | www.lecameleonhotel.com | Expensive)* offers intimate luxury, and is the region's first 5-star accommodation. The design is minimalist, and a dramatic contrast to the surrounding rainforest; white floors and walls, leather sofas and beds, complemented by wall hangings, throws and cushions in strong colours.

Well worth a visit – especially with children – is the ⊛ INSIDER TIP *Centro de Rescate Jaguar (guided tours only Mon–Sat 9.30am and 11.30am | US$20 | Punta Cocles, 6 km/3.7 mi south of Puerto Viejo | www.jaguarrescue.com)* in Playa Chiquita, a rescue centre for orphaned and injured wild animals. Sweet: they also look after orphaned baby sloths.

TORTUGUERO

(125 E3) (🗺 K3) The boat slowly glides through the deep green water of ⭐ Tortuguero National Park, past mangroves and palm trees, with the sunlight breaking through the overhanging leaves, white ibis and parrots fly up, the air is full of a sweet humidity and the sounds of the jungle.

One of the most memorable experiences on a trip through Costa Rica is the drive through the 73 mi² of this national park.

It consists of a system of lagoons and canals that are travelled in the traditional tree trunk canoes as well as on bigger boats. The wildlife reserve is home to manatees and hundreds of bird species. Ocelot and jaguar hunt the inaccessible humid forests, and the temperatures around 30 °C/86 °F and frequent rainfall have created an exceptionally species-rich vegetation, even by Costa Rican standards.

Tortuga means tortoise, and in fact the park's beaches are a breeding ground for turtles. From July until October the pregnant females swim to the shore on moonlit nights to lay their eggs – including the 200 kg/440 lbs green sea turtle. Tortuguero (pop. 1,400) is accessible from Moín, 7 km/4.4 mi north-west of Limón, by boat on canals that run north parallel to the coast *(77 km/47.9 mi | approx. US$35)*. It is also possible to get here by water from Puerto Viejo de Sarapiquí and La Pavona (17 km/10.6 mi from Cariari, poor gravel road) and air *(US$114)* from San José to the airport at the turtle station.

SIGHTSEEING

BOAT TRIPS

A ride along the waterways is one of the best ways to experience the countryside. The branches of the palm trees hang

SAVING TURTLES

As the digging up and selling of turtle eggs is still widespread in Costa Rica, many tourists act as "rescuers". They dig up the eggs themselves shortly after they have been laid and take them to conservationists, who put them in enclosures to hatch and then take the hatchlings down to the water. On the Atlantic, the turtles start laying in July, although you have to expect to be attacked by commercial egg collectors.

The stars and name-givers of Tortuguero National Park: turtles

down to the water, exotic birds flit from shore to shore, and monkeys accompany the boats. The individual lodges all have boats of various sizes that they can use to explore the rivers, lagoons and canals of the national park. This is usually in small groups and with an experienced guide. However, it is also possible to hire smaller boats for individual excursions.

TURTLE BEACH ★

The park was opened in 1975 for the protection of the endangered green water turtle, the hawksbill turtle and the leatherback turtle. From July to October, the heavy creatures crawl onto the beach to lay their eggs in the sand. They return to the water before the merciless sun reappears. During the season, the various places of accommodation offer tours to sections of the beach where the curious can watch this spectacle without disturbing the turtles.

FOOD & DRINK

Almost all of the lodges have restaurants, and meals are usually included in the price. In Tortuguero Village: cafés, *sodas* and basic restaurants.

INSIDER TIP ▶ BUDDA CAFÉ

Sundowners, salads and pizzas, cool jetty ambience with a touch of Ibiza and a hippie feeling about it, although true followers of Buddha will disregard the "om's" as wall decorations. *Daily 11am–9pm | C/ Principal | 25 m/82 ft north of the jetty | tel. 27 09 80 84 | www.buddacafe.com | Moderate*

TAYLOR'S PLACE

THE place to be after sundown: candles, palm fronds gently rustling in the breeze, and delicious rum and coconut cocktails. Owner Ray Taylor serves the best shrimps and steaks (with tamarind sauce) in the region. *Daily 6pm–9pm | Little Street | Tortuguero Village | Moderate*

LEISURE & SPORTS

All the lodges and hotels offer observations (July-October) of the turtles' nocturnal laying of their eggs on the beach; please book your tour *(US$30, only with a guide)* at the *Information kiosk* (see information) in Tortuguero Village. The hotels also offer boat trips to the lagoons in the national park, and you'll find a selection of places to hire canoes and kayaks on the beach in Tortuguero Village.

WHERE TO STAY

Surrounded by water and palm trees and in the typical style of the country – wooden houses, some constructed on stilts, there are several lodges along the lagoons and canals of Tortuguero. Visitors usually book their three- to four-day stays including board through the travel agencies in San José. Transportation is by light aircraft or via the river system from Puerto Viejo de Sarapiquí. Those who arrive independently by boat will find a number of basic guesthouses in Parismina and Tortuguero.

CABINAS BALCÓN DEL MAR

On the beach and at the end of the village: inexpensive tiny *cabinas* with and without bathrooms, also multi-bed rooms, communal kitchen. Ideal for long-term visitors with a small budget. *8 rooms | Tortuguero Beach | 100 m/328 ft north of the water tank | tel. 27 09 81 24 | Budget*

MAWAMBA LODGE

This hotel is situated on a strip of land between Tortuguero lagoon and the Caribbean sea, both on the beach and

The best way to explore the dense jungle greenery of Tortuguero National Park is by boat

with a jetty in the jungle. *54 rooms | tel. 22 93 81 81 | www.grupomawamba.com | Moderate*

PACHIRA LODGE

Best location on a promontory opposite the village and at the entrance to the national park: this comfortable lodge offers accommodation with meals and excursions. It includes 35 acres of nature and information provided by local guides. *88 rooms | tel. 22 57 22 42 | www.pachiralodge.com | Expensive*

TORTUGA LODGE

A site for jungle romantics, palm-leaf-covered and with tropical orchids in the garden; hiking trail through the rainforest. *27 rooms | 10 minutes by boat from the national park opposite the turtle station | tel. 22 57 07 66 | www.tortugalodge.com | Moderate*

INFORMATION

One professional (but commercial) address for information is *Asoprotour (on the jetty | Tortuguero | tel. 27 67 08 36 | www.asoprotur.com)*.

WHERE TO GO

BARRA DEL COLORADO ★
(125 E2) (ω J2)

Turtles sun themselves on the shore, palm-sized butterflies and tiny birds flit from flower to flower, while capuchin monkeys tumble through the trees. There is a second jungle swamp region 25 north of Tortuguero, less well known and with far fewer visitors. It also consists of natural lagoons and canals that were joined together over 100 years ago; a reserve in the estuary area of the Río Colorado, which stretches north to Barra del Colorado near the border with Nicaragua.

The tiny village of Barra del Colorado is inhabited by the coloured population, and also has a small landing strip and a wide, white beach. The jungle starts right on the outskirts. The *Río Colorado Lodge (18 rooms | tel. 22 32 40 63 | www.riocoloradolodge.com | Expensive)* is situated right on the river, and collects its guests from San José; the focus here is on fishing. Also offers boat trips into the jungle. Individual arrivals are most atmospheric from Puerto Viejo Sarapiquí in a three- or four-hour boat trip along the rivers Sarapiquí, San Juan (border river to Nicaragua) and Colorado rivers.

INSIDER TIP PARISMINA
(125 F4) (ω K4)

Some 20 km/12.4 mi south-east of Tortuguero on the estuary of the eponymous river is this tiny settlement. You can get to Parismina by bus from the *Gran Terminal Caribe (San José | C/ Central/Av. 10–11)* to Siquirres. There, walk from the new bus station to the old one (200 m/656 ft), and take the bus to Caño Blanco. Water taxis *(2,000 colones, 15 min.)* will take you to Parismina. The settlement has a small landing strip, and is situated on the waterway between Moín and Tortuguero. Americans particularly appreciate it for the deep-sea fishing. The *tarpón,* season – a 2-m/6.6-ft long, 50 kg/110 lbs herring variety that usually occurs in giant shoals off the coast – is from January to May. The town only has expensive lodges for fishermen and basic accommodation for nature and turtle lovers: The INSIDER TIP *Esmeralda Lodge (6 rooms | tel. 83 95 36 63 | www.esmeraldalodge.com | Budget)* offers romantic accommodation surrounded by nature. For information on activities and tours with local guides go to *www.parismina.com*.

DISCOVERY TOURS

❶ COSTA RICA AT A GLANCE

START: ❶ Alajuela
END: ㉚ Refugio Nacional Vida Sil. Golfito

14 days
Driving time
40 hours

Distance:
➡ 2,000 km/1,243 mi

COSTS: 1,233,000 colones per person for accommodation, ferry, boat, hire car, meals

WHAT TO PACK: Hiking boots, rain jacket, swimming things

IMPORTANT TIPS: In the rainy season, hire a car with 4-wheel drive; perhaps book an ultralight in ⑮ Playa Sámara

Would you like to explore the places that are unique to this region? Then the Discovery Tours are just the thing for you – they include terrific tips for stops worth making, breathtaking places to visit, selected restaurants and fun activities. It's even easier with the Touring App: download the tour with map and route to your smartphone using the QR Code on pages 2/3 or from the website address in the footer below – and you'll never get lost again even when you're offline.

TOURING APP

→ p. 2/3

Cloud jungle walks and swimming in volcanic mud, the Playa Sámara from a bird's-eye view and crocodiles in the river: although this circular tour includes the most impressive and best-known places in Costa Rica, it also never fails to provide exceptional perspectives of the land and people.

In the morning **walk around the centre of the colonial town of** ① Alajuela → p. 32 **to the** Parque Central **and its** cathedral, **explore the surrounding roads** and have a look at the patios. You'll learn all about the nation's heroes at the Museo Histórico Cultural Juan Santamaría

DAY 1

① Alajuela

🏧 🚻 🏠 🏛 🍴

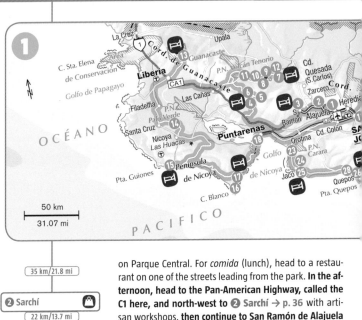

```
50 km
31.07 mi
```

PACIFICO

---

35 km/21.8 mi

② Sarchí 🛍

22 km/13.7 mi

③ La Posada de San Ramón 🛏

DAY 2–3

104.5 km/65 mi

④ Santa Elena 🍴🛏🏠🚶🏊

5.5 km/3.4 mi

⑤ Monteverde Cloud Forest Reserve 🏠🏠🚶

DAY 4–5

5.5 km/3.4 mi

⑥ Santa Elena 🛏

110 km/68 mi

⑦ La Fortuna 🛏

18 km/11.2 mi

⑧ Arenal Volcano 🏠🚶🏊

13.5 km/8.4 mi

---

on Parque Central. For *comida* (lunch), head to a restaurant on one of the streets leading from the park. **In the afternoon, head to the Pan-American Highway, called the C1 here, and north-west to ② Sarchí → p. 36** with artisan workshops, **then continue to San Ramón de Alajuela north of the C1 and the hotel ③ La Posada de San Ramón** (33 rooms | Av. 9/C/1 | tel. 24 45 73 59 | www.posadahotel. net | *Moderate*), where you will spend the night.

Continue west along the **Pan-American Highway, then north at Barranca, and at Rancho Grande branch right to Santa Elena** (partly a gravel track; 4WD required in the rainy season). Rainforests and cloud forest are the main features of the nature reserve around **Monteverde → p. 56**. The small town of **④ Santa Elena → p. 56** has inexpensive guest houses, romantic lodges and organic restaurants. You can explore the region here: check out the treetops from hanging bridges and explore the jungle on foot – perhaps on a (guided) night hike. The **⑤ Monteverde Cloud Forest Reserve** (www.cloudforestmonteverde.com) is east of Santa Elena, and if you go to the information centre they will explain the *trails* to you.

After your second night in **⑥ Santa Elena continue through Tilarán to ⑦ La Fortuna**. Choose your accommodation – the town is a base for exploration, perhaps of **⑧ Arenal Volcano → p. 53** and the fabulous surround-

ing nature. Splashing around in the **9 thermal pools** → p. 54 (Balnearios) heated by the active volcano is pure wellness. **10 Lake Arenal** → p. 53 is *the* place for wind-surfing, with offers and schools appropriate to its popularity. A visit to the **11 La Pequeña Helvecia** *(daily | Nuevo Arenal/north shore | Lake Arenal | tel. 26 92 80 12 | www. pequenahelvecia.com)*, is an experience: known as "mini Switzerland", you'll not only find rösti, but cow stalls, a chapel and a cable car as well. Itchy feet? Then explore the surrounding national parks.

From **12 La Fortuna** drive north-west through Liberia → p. 50 to **13 Rincón de la Vieja National Park** → p. 54. A visit is a must! Overnight on the outskirts of the park at the **Hacienda Guachipelin** → p. 55. Unbeatable: a bath in volcanic mud.

Back to Liberia, then take the Carretera 21 south, via Santa Cruz → p. 61 and Nicoya → p. 62 – stop in **14 Guaitil** → p. 61, to hunt for ceramics – **and to 15 Playa Sámara** → p. 63 to find that night's accommodation. You might feel like arranging for a microlight from **Flying Crocodile** to fly you over the jungle and beach.

Right down south is **Montezuma** → p. 61. **The hiking in the nearby 16 Reserva Natural Cabo Blanco** is the perfect counterbalance to the beach. Spend the night at the **17 Hotel Aurora** *(20 rooms | Northern outskirts | Mon-*

9 Thermal pools

12.5 km/7.8 mi

10 Lake Arenal

14 km/8.7 mi

11 La Pequeña Helvecia

DAY 6

31 km/19.3 mi

12 La Fortuna

165 km/103 mi

13 Rincón de la Vieja National Park

DAY 7

101 km/63 mi

14 Guaitil

97 km/60.3 mi

15 Playa Sámara

DAY 8

94 km/58.4 mi

16 Reserva Natural Cabo Blanco

9 km/5.6 mi

tezuma | tel. 26 42 00 51 | www.hotelaurora-montezuma. com | Budget–Moderate) only 100 m/328 ft from the beach.

Carretera 160 runs north to Paquera, where you take the ferry *(www.nicoyapeninsula.com)* to Puntarenas → p. 72. After lunch on the ⑱ Paseo de los Turistas → p. 73 head to the capital ⑲ San José → p. 45, where you will also spend the night. A visit to the Museo del Oro Precolombino is compulsory. The Museum of Gold has thousands of figurines and jewellery from pre-Columbian times.

On the way from San José to the Caribbean port Puerto Limón → p. 78 you'll pass the ⑳ Parque Nacional Braulio Carrillo → p. 45 and the Río Sucio (dirty river). You can watch a famous spectacle from a bridge over the Carretera 32: the confluence of the clear Río Honduras and the Río Sucio, which springs from the volcano Irazú. Its iron and sulphur deposits colour the water a rusty red. A few hundred metres on from the confluence, the colour of the Río Sucio changes to green. Continue driving to the port of Moín north of Puerto Limón. Leave your car in a monitored car park, and take a boat to ㉑ Tortuguero National Park → p. 84, known for its lagoon and canal landscape, its biodiversity and its rare tropical plants. You can be sure of a pleasant stay at the Cabinas Balcón del Mar → p. 86.

Back from Tortuguero, drive from Puerto Limón along the Caribbean coast via Cahuita and head south. Relaxed Caribbean beach and party life calls in ㉒ Puerto Viejo de Talamanca → p. 83.

Travelling through San José, it'll take you 6–7 hours to get back to the Pacific coast to Jacó. On the way, stop at the ㉓ bridge at Tárcoles to photograph the lazy crocodiles lying on the shore. A little further along, take the gondola of the ㉔ Rainforest Aerial Tramway → p. 71 and glide over a waterfall into the jungle. Spend the night in ㉕ Jacó → p. 69.

Drive on to ㉖ Quepos → p. 74 and move into your quarters for the night. One highlight is ㉗ Manuel Antonio National Park → p. 75. You'll find monkeys and parrots here – and light sandy beaches. A boat ride from Quepos to the

㉘ **Isla Damas** → p. 74 will see you among the birds of a mangrove forest.

As you continue **on to Golfito** you'll drive past light sandy and dark gravel beaches, through jungle and palm oil plantations. The climate will become increasingly humid, the vegetation tropical. You'll see palm trees, bananas and orchids. The tiny port of ㉙ **Golfito** → p. 64, between the bay and the green hills of the ㉚ **Refugio Nacional de Vida Silvestre Golfito** → p. 66, attracts with walks around the nearby rainforest and boat trips out to distant (surfer) beaches.

14 km/8.7 mi

㉘ Isla Damas

DAY 14

169 km/105 mi

㉙ Golfito

2.5 km/1.6 mi

㉚ Refugio Nacional de Vida Silvestre Golfito

---

② FROM SAN JOSÉ THROUGH NATIONAL PARKS TO THE CARIBBEAN COAST

START: ① San José
END: ⑤ Barra del Colorado National Park

Distance:
approx. 150 km/93 mi

3 days
Driving time
4.5 hours

COSTS: 171,250 colones per person for accommodation, meals, cable car, bus, boat
WHAT TO PACK: Rain jacket, swimming things, hiking boots

IMPORTANT TIPS: Don't forget your passport!

From San José you can easily get to the national park on the Caribbean coast using public transport: by bus, a short ride on the gondola through the jungle treetops, and then an exciting boat ride.

From the bus station Terminal del Caribe *(C/ Central/Av. 13–15)* in ① **San José** → p. 45 **take the early morning bus via Guápiles to Cariari, and start off with the** ② **Braulio Carrillo National Park** → p. 45. Shortly after going through the Zurquí Tunnel the bus crosses the **Río Sucio** → p. 44. A few minutes later (5 km/3.1 mi past the bridge) on the right is the access to the almost legendary **Rainforest Aerial Tramway** → p. 44, known by the locals as the *teleférico* "cable car". Leave the bus and enjoy the ride through the jungle. Allow at least three hours. Once you have arrived, a cable car employee will help you find the

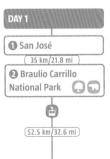

DAY 1

① San José

35 km/21.8 mi

② Braulio Carrillo National Park

52.5 km/32.6 mi

❸ Hotel El Trópico 🛏

DAY 2–3

47 km/29.2 mi

❹ Puerto Lindo de
Pococí 🚢

1.5 km/0.9 mi

correct bus to Cariari. **At Guápiles the Ruta 247 branches off north to Cariari. Spend the night at the** ❸ **Hotel El Trópico** *(20 rooms | Barrio Palermo | tel. 27 67 71 86 | www. hoteltropico.com | Budget)*.

From Cariari take the 2pm bus to ❹ **Puerto Lindo de Pococí 47 km/29.2 mi to the north**– a very exciting ride through the wilderness and jungle that takes about 2–3 hours. **The bus will deposit you at the harbour pier, where flat motor boats will be waiting for the hour-long trip through the canals of the Río Colorado and Barra del Colorado National Park.** Have US$5 ready to cross the Río San Juan, the border river to Nicaragua (you'll need your

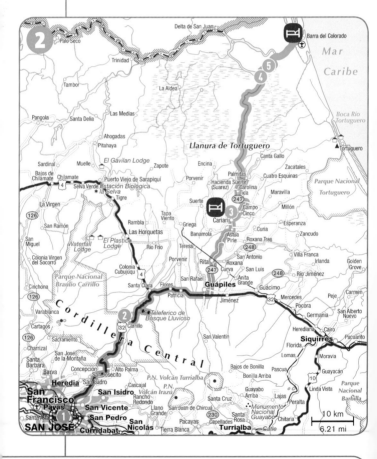

Adventure jungle: through the canals of the Barra del Colorado National Park

passport) and US$10 for admission to the ❺ **Barra del Colorado National Park** → p. 87 on the Nicaraguan border. **The boat goes to the village of Barra del Colorado on the left shore of the river, where the staff at your accommodation, the** Silver King Lodge *(23 | tel. 84 47 59 88 | www.silverkinglodge.com | Expensive)***, will collect you**. The lodge provides INSIDER TIP free canoes and kayaks for tours of the national park. The next day is full of hikes and paddling on the rivers, canals and lagoons. You will be awoken by the noises of the jungle, learn all sorts of interesting things about the nature on a guided tour, and get close views of howler monkeys, turtles and crocodiles.

❺ Barra del Colorado National Park

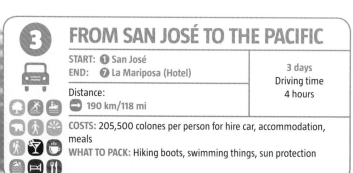

③ FROM SAN JOSÉ TO THE PACIFIC

START: ❶ San José	
END: ❼ La Mariposa (Hotel)	3 days Driving time 4 hours
Distance: 🚗 190 km/118 mi	

COSTS: 205,500 colones per person for hire car, accommodation, meals
WHAT TO PACK: Hiking boots, swimming things, sun protection

From the darkly glowing Pacific beaches to the white playas of the national park, surrounded by jungle and wild animals: from Jacó, you travel along the Pacific to Quepos and the Manuel Antonio National Park.

DAY 1

① San José

(89.5 km/55.6 mi)

② Parque Nacional Carara

23 km/14.3 mi

③ Playa de Jacó

On the motorway you'll travel west from **①** San José → p. 45 through the Valle Central and the little town of Orotina. A few more miles to the south is the beginning of the **②** Parque Nacional Carara → p. 69, home to jaguars, pumas and ocelots. Look forward to monkeys and wonderfully coloured tropical birds, including giant ara parrots. Trails take you further into the national park. And shortly after it's "Welcome to Jacó". The beaches of **③** Playa de Jacó → p. 71 radiate a party atmosphere. Waves are high and prices low, making Jacó *the* destination even for young wind surfers. Don't miss the chance for a walk across the mudflats when the tide is out – you might come across some *sanddollars*. After sunset head to the Bar Nirvana *(daily 7pm–2am | Av. Pastor Diaz | tel. 84 29 52 55)* for live reggae and rock music. Later on you'll find a bed for the night at the Mar de Luz → p. 72.

DAY 2–3

67 km/41.6 mi

④ Quepos

The road continues, crosses the river of the same name at Parrita and wends its way land inwards for a few miles before ending in a bay at **④** Quepos → p. 74 , the destination of this journey. Find somewhere to stay and then go to Cambute Tours *(tel. 27 77 32 29 | mangrovetour.com)* for a boat ride through the canals of the Isla Damas estuary. Keep a close eye on your bag – little monkeys might hop on-board as you pass under trees. **A narrow road**

To end the day, an evening meal with a view: La Mariposa

You can find these tours as an app at: **go.marco-polo.com/cri**

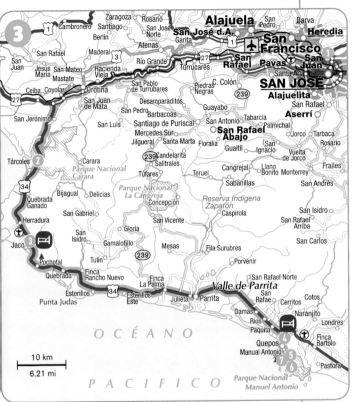

winds its way from Quepos 7 km/4.4 mi up the mountain and back down again. There are restaurants and lodges in tropical gardens on the slopes on both sides of the road. You'll have a panoramic view of the national park and its islands from ⑤ **Emilio's Café** *(Closed Tuesdays | Ctra. a Manuel Antonio, km 4/mi 2.5/near Plaza Vista Shopping | tel. 27 77 68 07 | Moderate)*. Next day you'll have the chance to explore the famous ⑥ **Manuel Antonio National Park → p. 75.** **At the end of the road before you get to the park is the Manuel Antonio settlement.** Along the riverside road, which is only a sandy track here, long-term travellers sit in the cafés as Indian batiks and amulets flap in the wind. End the day up on the terrace of ⑦ **La Mariposa hotel → p. 76:** with the sea and national park at your feet. Fabulous!

4.5 km/2.8 mi

⑤ Emilio's Café

3 km/1.9 mi

⑥ Manuel Antonio National Park

3 km/1.9 mi

⑦ La Mariposa

4
ON FOOT THROUGH THE CURI-CANCHA CLOUD FOREST

START: ❶ Santa Elena
END: ❶ Santa Elena

1 day
Actual walking time
4 hours

Distance: very easy
🚶 4 km/2.5 mi ▪▮▮ Height: 180 m/590 ft

COSTS: US$26 per person (bus, admission charges), possibly a guide for 3 hours US$45, taxi US$8
WHAT TO PACK: Hiking boots, water

IMPORTANT TIPS: Only 50 people are allowed into Curi-Cancha at a time, so be at the entrance as early as possible!

Of all the nature reserves around Santa Elena and Monteverde, the little-visited private Refugio de Vida Silvestre Curi-Cancha is particularly lovely. After the hike it's on to the "Bat jungle".

❶ Santa Elena

2.5 km/1.6 mi

❷ Stella's Bakery

500 m/1640 ft

❸ Reserva Curi-Cancha

3 km/1.9 mi

07:30am Take the shuttle bus from ❶ **Santa Elena** → p. 56 to Monteverde → p. 56 and get off at Casem, a women's co-operative for art and crafts. Fortify yourself with breakfast at ❷ **Stella's Bakery** *(daily from 7am | tel. 26 45 55 60 | Budget)* across the road. Then walk along the gravel road **that heads west between Stella's Bakery and the Cheese Factory** *(opposite the Casem souvenir shop)* **and branches off to the Curi-Cancha nature reserve.** The ❸ **Reserva Curi-Cancha** *(US$12, guide US$15 per hour | tel. 26 45 69 15 | www.reservacuricancha.com)* is open daily from 7am–4pm, and from 6pm–8pm for night hikes *(caminata nocturna)*.

09:00am Six signposted trails cover the hilly terrain, **take the path to the Mirador a la División Continental lookout**. A guided tour (3 hours) is recommended. This way, you will get to see all the things you would have missed, such as the roots of a strangler fig, singing bellbirds, rare quetzals in avocado trees, toucans, or spider monkeys tumbling around the treetops. From the **Mirador a la División Continental** you can see over the continental water divide: to the west, rivers flow into the Pacific, to the east into the Atlantic. After three hours – full of information, short breaks, looking for things with binoculars – you'll be back at the entrance.

12:00pm Lunch is at **4 Casem** → p. 59. Then it's on to the **5 Bat Jungle** (*daily 9am–7.30pm | Tour US$12 | tel. 26 45 77 01 | www.batjungle.com*) **nearby and behind Stella's Bakery**. A large darkened room is home to some 90 bats, and you can get right up close to them on a 45-minute tour. Back into the sun and rummage through the shelves at **6 Casem** → p. 59 for that INSIDER TIP exceptional souvenir for your friends at home. And if you miss the last shuttle bus back to **1 Santa Elena**, one of the nice señoritas of Casem will be pleased to call you a taxi.

4 Casem 🍴

 150 m/492 ft

5 Bat Jungle

 150 m/492 ft

6 Casem

 2.5 km/1.6 mi

1 Santa Elena

Like a different world: mysterious cloud forest

SPORTS & ACTIVITIES

Costa Rica is the perfect destination for sporty nature-lovers. Whether trekking through the stunning rainforest, kayak tours and river-rafting in fast-flowing rivers, riding out across a black shimmering lava beach or diving amongst the turtles and barracudas, the offer is extensive, but prices are always moderate.

Conditions along the Atlantic and Pacific coasts are also excellent for water sports. Costa Rica's national parks are unique, and there a several different ways to explore them. Twenty small tourism providers have got together to make up the INSIDER TIP *Turismo Rural Comunitario (tel. 22 34 70 02 | www.actuarcostarica.com)* and offer eco holidays and tours.

ADVENTURE SPORTS

For a Tarzan feeling amongst tree-houses and lianas, go for one of the *canopy tours* that are rapidly increasing in Costa Rica. You'll walk through the treetops in the rainforest using a system of hanging bridges, or glide through the nature attached to steel cables. There are now over 100 providers.

The *Adventure Park (www.adventureparkcostarica.com)* of Finca Daniel near Puntarenas on the outskirts of a large private forest with views of the Gulf of Nicoya is perfect for a short active holiday. As well 25 zip lines for gliding through the canopy, passing over 11 waterfalls *(3 hours, US$99, also shorter tours)* and horse-riding into the jungle,

 Photo: Playa Santa Teresa

Two coasts and numerous rivers for water sports, and the natural parks aren't just a challenge for hikers

there is an excitingly constructed system of hanging bridges, steps, ladders and ropes that takes you up high into the treetops. At the *ATV Fun Park,* the form of transportation is quad bikes, and you can choose from various levels of difficulty.

DIVING & SNORKELLING

On the north end of the west coast, the volcanic islands Islas Catalinas rise up steeply from the sandy ocean floor to around 30 m/98.4 ft. Among the sights you'll see are rays, barracudas, sharks, moray eels and turtles. INSIDER TIP *Costa Rica Diving (Playa Flamingo | 450 m/1,476 ft before the Flamingo/Potrero junction | tel. 26 54 41 48 | www.cos tarica-diving.com),* a diving school with equipment and training to qualify offers accompanied diving courses to 30 diving sites at depths of between 15 and 40 m/49.2 and 131.2 ft (visibility up to 30 m/98.4 ft).

Although the coral reefs of the Caribbean coast are suitable for snorkelling, the currents are often so strong that you won't see much in the churned up water. However, the beaches on the Pacific are also ideal for snorkelling, as there are several small bays among the rocks between the sandy sections that are home to fish and crustaceans and which you can observe.

GOLF

Golf in the Tropics? Particularly appealing for the diversity of the plant life, say the experts. If you play as soon as the sun rises, the climate is pleasant with a lovely light, and at the most the birds as your companions. The country has a number of golf courses, the loveliest of which is the *Cariari Country Club (18 holes, par 71, 6,260 m/20,538 ft | www. clubcariari.com)* of the Meliá Cariari hotel in San José. Information is available on the websites and elsewhere *www. golfincostarica.com* and *www.teetimes costarica.com*.

HORSE RIDING

Hotels and ranches have suitable mounts, and offer guided hacks around the country. Better avoid the poor creatures that spend the whole day in the sun, standing sadly on the beach and are available for an hourly rate of US$10.

PARAGLIDING

Costa Rica from above, over the ocean and jungle: paragliding has become very popular. There are plenty of cliffs to launch from and landing places on the beach, especially at Caldera and Turrialba. Beginners start with a tandem flight. Circular trips, either as part of a group or individual, are offered by *Skyhigh (www. skyhigh-costarica.com)*.

RIVER-RAFTING & KAYAK

Wild-water rides are possible in several different parts of the country. An

Volcano Arenal: worthwhile destination for riders and walkers – even though you're not allowed to climb up it

experienced skipper guides the dinghy over rapids and small waterfalls, and if you're on a trip of a few days you'll stay in a tent beside the river. You can choose from river sections of different levels of difficulty, as appropriate to your age, skills and experience, and there are even suitable tours for children. One recommended provider is e.g. *Ríos Tropicales (C/ 38 351 | tel. 22 33 64 55 | www.riostropicales.com)* in San José.

STAND-UP PADDLING

Trendy SUP is also pretty hip in Costa Rica. Almost all of the windsurfing schools and board shops have the equipment to hire, as do a number of the beach hotels in Jacó and – very often – on Nicoya Peninsula (e.g. Playa Tamarindo, Playa Sámara). Lessons are available, including in SUP yoga – why not try it? It's tremendous fun! – from *Costa Rica Stand up Paddle Adventures (Tamarindo | www.costaricasupadventures.com)*.

SURFING

On the Pacific coast, beginners are advised to try the beach at Jacó, because you can hire the equipment there and you'll be supervised. Advanced surfers go to the beaches of Nosara, Tamarindo or Sámara. On the Atlantic coast, surfers are most frequently seen at Puerto Viejo de Talamanca and Punta Uva.

TREKKING

You really must pack your hiking boots, because Costa Rica's species-rich nature is best experienced on foot. The palette ranges from an hour-long stroll through the Manuel Antonio National Park to several days' trekking with local guides through the trackless rainforest where

you'll pitch your own tent for the night. The Corcovado and Rincón de la Vieja national parks provide plenty of adventures and thrills – and have the most species-rich eco system in the country. The providers include *Osa Aventura (www.osa aventura.com/guided-corcovado-treks)* and *Aventuras Tierra Verde (www.adven ture-costarica.com)*.

WELLNESS

Wellness for body and mind, yoga and meditation are also popular in Costa Rica. The Americans were mainly responsible for introducing the awareness for this side of life into the country, and now offer rainforest and ocean retreats, run yoga studios and wellness hostels. One well-known address is *Nosara Wellness (www.nosarawellness.com)* on the Nicoya Peninsula. Reiki masters, acupuncturists and qualified masseurs offer a wide range of treatments and healing methods. The *Holis Wellness Center (www.spaholis.com)* at Manuel Antonio with wonderful surroundings offers yoga courses, Pilates and wellness treatments, carried out by qualified specialists who are extremely enthusiastic about what they do. Whether detox body cleanse, yoga or meditation, the *Pacha Mama* (see p. 63) is run with love and commitment by followers of Osho, and is steadily growing.

WINDSURFING

There is now special accommodation for windsurfers at the Laguna de Arenal with its constant breezes. The neighbouring *Lago de Coter* also attracts lots of surfers. On the Pacific side, there are windsurfers on the beaches at Tambor, Flamingo, Potrero and Tamarindo as well as on the Golfo Dulce.

TRAVEL WITH KIDS

Costa Ricans love children, have lots of *niños* themselves, and they are integrated smoothly in everyday life. And then there's the nature: waterfalls, real volcanoes, a river with crocodiles, the rainforest – Costa Rica is just one great, big jungle book for children. A few points to remember: as the quality of the water in the pools of small hotels might not be the best, ear plugs should be worn to prevent the risk of infection. The monkeys that swing through all the trees are a particular delight for children because they come up close and want to be fed. However, the animals can become aggressive if they don't get as much as they want or what they want. Parents should therefore be present at all times if their children are feeding the monkeys – or, better still, don't feed them at all.

A significant proportion of the country's mid-class hotels have European or American owners. They are well organised, a little more expensive that the local hotels, and are often preferred by tourists, not least because of the ease of communication. INSIDER TIP Anyone travelling with children should, whenever possible, visit the hotels of the *ticos*: children receive a much warmer welcome and are generally much better looked after there.

CENTRAL PLATEAU

INSIDER TIP MUSEO DE LOS NIÑOS
(U D2) (*ʃ d2*)

The interactive "children's museum" in San José offers many attractions and activities in its 33 rooms and outside. Children will experience a dairy farm and an earthquake, and learn how an orchestra and space travel work. *Tue–Fri 8am–4pm, Sat/Sun 9.30am–5pm | 2,200 colones, children to age 15 2,000 colones | C/4/Av. 9 | www.museocr.org*

RAINFOREST AERIAL TRAMWAY
(125 D5) (*ʃ H4*)

Once they are five years old, children can float between the rainforest treetops provided they are accompanied by an adult. First, though, they are shown a video so they know what to expect – but the reality is far more exciting. *Daily 8am–4pm | US$65, children US$32 | between San José and Guápiles, 5 km/3.1 mi past the Río Sucio | www.rainforestadventure.com*

SPIROGYRA BUTTERFLY GARDEN (JARDÍN DE MARIPOSAS)
(U E2) (*ʃ e2*)

As it is a little smaller than the other butterfly farms in the country – although

Travelling with children is a pleasure in Costa Rica – and not just on the beach or because of the monkeys at breakfast

every bit as diverse – the Butterfly Garden in the capital San José is perfect for visiting with children. *Mon–Fri 9am–2pm, Sat/Sun 9am–3pm | US$7, children US$5 | 50 m/164 ft east and 150 m/492 ft south of the El Pueblo Shopping Center | www.butterflygardencr.com*

THE NORTH-WEST

BOSQUE ETERNO DE LOS NIÑOS (CHILDREN'S ETERNAL RAIN FOREST)
(123 E4) (*ŵ E4*)

In the year 1986 the jungle region in Monteverde gained considerable international fame thanks to the "Children's Rainforest" project for which children in a total of 44 countries collected donations. Of course, the Children's Rainforest also has a child-appropriate visitor centre and an educational trail for children. *Daily 8am–5pm | US$12, children free | Access "Bajo del Tigre" | 3.5 km/2.2 mi southeast of Santa Elena on the road to Monteverde | www.acmcr.org*

RAINSONG WILDLIFE SANCTUARY 🕲
(126 B4) (*ŵ D6*)

At the southern end of Nicoya Peninsula is the Wildlife Rescue Center that cares for injured and poorly animals, from monkeys to turtles. As well as horse-riding trips and bird-watching tours *(each US$20)* the centre also collects donations. *Daily 8am–11am and 2pm–5pm | Donation US$5 | Cabuya | www.rainsong sanctuary.com*

PACIFIC COAST

PARQUE MARINO DEL PACÍFICO
(123 E6) (*ŵ E5*)

Learning is demonstrated clearly here: tomorrow's "marine biologists" will find a crocodile nursery, lots of turtles and tropical fish in Puntarenas. Expert information is also provided. *Tue–Sun 9am–4.30pm | US$10, children to age 11 US$5 | Old station | 500 m/1,640 ft east of the cruise ship pier | www.par quemarino.org*

FESTIVALS & EVENTS

If you make a pilgrimage to the Lady of the Angels or prefer to celebrate the traditional Festival of the Little Devils or the carnival – there's certainly plenty of variety in Costa Rica. The most important day of the year is Easter.

2 FEBRUARY

Día de la Candelaria (Candlemas) is celebrated with particular style in Paraíso near Cartago; there are plays, concerts, music and dance in honour of the Virgin.

FEBRUARY

Lots of towns celebrate the **INSIDER TIP** *Fiesta de los Diablitos* in February, the "Festival of the Little Devils" when, to the accompaniment of flutes and drums, the locals present imaginatively designed balsa wood masks they have made to commemorate the battles between the indigenous people and the Spanish a long time ago. The Spaniards are represented by bulls, the native by *diablitos* (little devils).
Young men clamber into the arena and attempt to escape the high-spirited young bulls: from the end of February until the beginning of March, the 11 days of the *Fiestas Cívicas* take place in the provincial capital of Liberia, a folk festival with horseback processions, a cattle market, lots of folklore, bull riding and a beauty contest.

MIDDLE OF APRIL

The *Festival Internacional de las Artes* has music performances and plays, ballet and other dancing all over San José, and a craft market on the Plaza de la Cultura.

EASTER

Ever since colonial times, **Easter** has been the most important festival in Costa Rica, and is celebrated across the country with processions. Those who can, enjoy a mini break for the **Semana Santa**, Easter week.

MIDDLE OF JULY

The *Fiesta de la Virgen del Mar*, the festive procession to honour the Virgin of the Sea, takes place on the water at Puntarenas.
Almost every kind of seagoing vessel takes part, from simple rowing boats to motor yachts, all beautifully decorated and illuminated. Thus adorned, the

water parade processes once around the peninsula in the Gulf of Nicoya. *www.puntarenas.com/puntarenas/virgendelmar.html*

2 AUGUST
On **Our Lady of the Angels Day** crowds of pilgrims proceed to the basilica in Cartago, where Nuestra Señora de los Ángeles, Our Lady of the Angels, appeared in 1635 and became the country's patron saint.

OCTOBER
Weeks before the actual date on 12 October you'll hear the steel drums practising for the big procession. And then come the week of the ★ **Carnival in Limón**, you can forget about getting any sleep as the Limonenses stroll through the streets accompanied by samba-loving visitors.

20 DECEMBER–2 JANUARY
Between Christmas and New Year, ★ **Fin del Año** is celebrated, the end of the year, with horse parades *(topes)*, bullfights *(corridas)* and festive processions, particularly elaborately in the centre of San José.

PUBLIC HOLIDAYS

1 Jan	*Año Nuevo* (New Year's Day)
19 March	*Día de San José*
9/10 April 20, 1/2 April 21, 14/15 April 22	*Jueves y Viernes Santo* (Maundy Thursday/ Good Friday)
11 April	*Juan-Santamaría*
1 May	*Día del Trabajo*
29 June	*San Pedro y Pablo*
25 July	*Anexión de Guanacaste*
2 Aug.	*Virgen de los Ángeles*
15 Aug	*Día de la Madre* (Assumption Day/ Mothering Sunday)
15 Sept	*Día de la Independencia* (Independence Day)
12 Oct	*Día de la Raza* (Columbus Day)
2 Nov	*Día de los Muertos*
8 Dec	*Concepción Inmaculada* (Immaculate Conception)
25 Dec	*Navidad* (Christmas)

LINKS, BLOGS, APPS & MORE

LINKS & BLOGS

www.turismo-sostenible.co.cr Useful list of travel agents and hotels from all over the country that hold Certification for Sustainable Tourism from the Costa Rican tourism authority

https://www.ef.edu/pg/student-exchange/costa-rica/ Different foreign exchange programmes for high school, college, or university students, adults and professionals

https://www.visitcostarica.com/en Official website for tourism in Costa Rica – has information on everything ranging from ecotourism to honeymoons in Costa Rica

https://greenglobaltravel.com/ecotourism-in-costa-rica/ "The Ultimate Eco Travel Guide" for Costa Rica, includes a travel blog

www.vozdeguanacaste.com Forum with insider news from Nosara, Sámara, Nicoya and on the beaches of Nicoya Peninsula

www.costarica.com/blog Impressive travel descriptions on the country's various regions and various topics in the Costa Rica travel blog

blog.therealcostarica.com Everything about living and daily life in Costa Rica – for the curious, for travellers and even for pensioners

twoweeksincostarica.com Blog with a variety of content on what to do in Costa Rica

short.travel/cri4 Travelling alone as woman, various travel routes and much more: the community shares traveller tips and rates travelling in Costa Rica

Regardless of whether you are still researching your trip or already in Costa Rica: these addresses will provide you with more information, videos and networks to make your holiday even more enjoyable

www.internations.org/costa-rica-expats Tips and news from expats living in Costa Rica

https://costarriquenismos.soft112.com Learn words and phrases that are part of every conversation in Costa Rica and will help you to quickly make contact with the ticos and their world. You could say genuine tico slang

VIDEOS

short.travel/cri1 A 7-minute video tour of the capital with plenty of the sights – even if they are only seen in passing

www.travelvideo.com/destinations/costa-rica/video Several short videos on the country's nature parks, animals and birds, and the stone spheres

https://www.youtube.com/watch?v=NKpF_avJ71o A fascinating documentary filmed in 5 different locations in Costa Rica on wildlife and more

APPS

Costa Rica ¡Pura Vida! The iPhone app to towns and beaches, restaurants and activities

Bird sounds of Costa Rica! Over 2,000 tracks with some 800 special of Costa Rican birds

Costa Rica Birds Field Guide The Birds' Field Guide is available as an app for Android. Not only will you hear the sounds of the jungle birds, but there's also information on which birds you will find where in Costa Rica and how you can go about hearing as many of them as possible

TRAVEL TIPS

ADDRESSES

Not all the streets have names, and instead you'll see something like "100 m south of xy park". House numbers are virtually unknown, and the corner is given instead: Av. 4/C/5, i.e. Avenida 4, corner Calle 5, or in writing e.g. C/ 2/ Av. 2–4 (even shorter: c2, a2/4): "2nd road between Avenidas 2 and 4". Otherwise, PO boxes are provided *(apartado, apto, apdo)*.

ARRIVAL

✈ Several airlines fly from London to San José and Liberia with travel times ranging from around eleven to 24 hours. British Airways offers some direct flights *(www.britishairways.com)*. Many different airlines (Delta, United, American, …) offer flights for example from New York, Los Angeles, or Chicago to Costa Rica. The non-stop ones from United to San José are usually under six hours. You can get non-stop flights from Montreal and Toronto, for example with Air Canada, which also takes slightly more than five hours.

The airport taxi (orange, ticket from the desk in the Arrivals hall) to San José costs 8,200–10,300, to Heredia 10,300 and to Alajuela 3,400 colones, by bus (change your money into colones at the airport!) is less than 700 colones.

BANKS & CHANGING MONEY

Costa Rica's currency is the colón (with 100 céntimos), and it suffers greatly from inflation. Prices are therefore given in US$, and increasingly also in the countryside, where the dollar is practically the second currency and is used as the base for the exchange rate. Even smaller towns have ATMs that accept international bank cards. Banks are open from 9am–3pm Mon–Fri. Credit cards (Visa, Amex) are widely used. The current exchange rate is available e.g. at *www.oanda.com*

RESPONSIBLE TRAVEL

It doesn't take a lot to be environmentally friendly whilst travelling. Don't just think about your carbon footprint whilst flying to and from your holiday destination but also about how you can protect nature and culture abroad. As a tourist it is especially important to respect nature, look out for local products, cycle instead of driving, save water and much more. If you would like to find out more about eco-tourism please visit: *www.ecotourism.org*

CAMPING

The administration office of the national parks has a brochure on camping in the nature reserves, as does the ICT. However, camping in the national parks is increasingly being restricted, although more and more private sites are opening up, mainly on beaches.

CAR HIRE

Hire cars are available from about US$200–250 per week (without taxes and insurance); a Range Rover will cost twice that. All flaws are entered on a check-list that you should check very carefully; they like to charge for scratches and dents when you return the vehicle. Recommended: *Payless Rent a Car (Paseo Colón /Calles 36–38 | San José | tel. 22 56 01 01 | www.paylesscr.com)*; there are also offices at the airport and in Liberia. *Adobe Cars (tel. 25 42 48 00 | www.adobecar.com)* has ten stations, and also has vehicles with all-wheel drive. Visitors who hire a car must also take out luggage insurance. Vehicles are often parked in monitored car parks. Although this "monitoring" won't always prevent a break-in, at least they are insured for any damage.

CLIMATE, WHEN TO GO

Temperatures are about the same all year round, with only minor fluctuations between the months. In the highlands the average temperature is around 22 °C/72 °F, on the coasts up to 30 °C/86 °F. The dry season in the highlands and on the Pacific side is from November to April. The peak travel season is therefore from December to April, with peaks at Christmas and Easter, and regionally also in July and August. Costa Rica's rainy season is from May until October. Although it usually only rains in the afternoons, they are pretty impressive downpours. It's humid at this time, and there are not many tourists about. This means prices are lower then, and lots of hotels have special offers. On the Caribbean side, you must also expect rain showers during the dry season.

Tips on travelling for nature and animal lovers: whales arrive on the Pacific coast in January, and lots of birds breed in March/April. Orchids flower in

BUDGETING

Coffee	£0.90–1.15/ US$1.15–1.50 *for one cup*
Snack	£1.30/US$1.75 *for one gallo*
Beer	£2/US$2.70 *for one bottle*
Hammock	£13–18/US$17–23 *for a cotton hamaca*
Petrol	around £0.90/ US$1.15 *for 1 l regular petrol*
National Park	£13/US$17.50 *for admission*

March, and the turtles come onto the beaches to lay their eggs between July and October.

CONSULATES AND EMBASSIES

BRITISH EMBASSY IN SAN JOSÉ
Edificio Centro Colón /Paseo Colón and Streets 38 and 40 / Apartado 815 – 1007 / *tel.* +506 2258 2025 (from Costa Rica) or 020 7008 1500 (from the UK) / https://www.gov.uk/world/organisations/british-embassy-in-costa-rica

U.S. EMBASSY IN SAN JOSÉ
Calle 98 Vía 104 / Pavas / tel. (506) 2519-2000 / https://cr.usembassy.gov/

EMBASSY OF CANADA IN SAN JOSÉ
Behind the "Contraloría" in the Oficentro Ejecutivo La Sabana / Building 5, Third floor / tel. 0 800 015 1161

CUSTOMS

It is permitted to bring 200 cigarettes and 3 litres of alcoholic beverages into Costa Rica, along with items for personal use, without paying duty. When returning to the EU the allowance includes 200 cigarettes, 1 litre of spirits, 500 g/1.1 lbs coffee and goods to a value of 430 euros (294,550 colon/£378); to the USA normally goods to a value of US$800; see www.cbp.gov for all details.

DOMESTIC FLIGHTS

The national airline is *Sansa Air (tel. 22 90 41 00 | www.flysansa.com)*, and it operates propeller aircraft (tickets US$50 –100) from the international airport of Juan Santamaría. The private airline *Nature Air (Aeropuerto Nacional Tobías Bolaños | Pavas | 4 km/2.5 mi west of San José | tel. 22 99 60 00 | www. natureair.com)* also offers lots of domestic flights. You can also book online with a credit card.

DRIVING

A national licence is sufficient for holiday visitors. When driving off the main roads and in national parks you'll need a vehicle with four-wheel drive *(doble tracción)*. Some of the roads are very poor, even dangerous. There are no signposts, and the *ticos* drive recklessly. Do not go out in the dark. Speed limit: 80 km/h/50 mph, and 90 km/h/55 mph on the road from San José–Puerto Limón.

ELECTRICITY

110 volt, US flat plugs

EMERGENCY SERVICES

General emergency (tel. 9 11 | also in English). Red Cross (tel. 128)

HEALTH

Costa Rica is largely free of epidemic diseases, and medical care in the capital is excellent. In an emergency: *Clínica Bíblica (Av. 14/C/ Central–1 | tel. 25 22 10 00 | www.clinicabiblica.com)*. Inoculations are not required for a visit. There is a risk of malaria and dengue fever in coastal areas and in regions below

PARADISE FOR ESCAPISTS

Over the past three decades, numerous visitors to the country have decided not to go home. They came originally from Europe or North America, bought property in Costa Rica and found a source of income: a small hotel, a few guest bungalows, a restaurant, a diving, riding or flying school, or even an entire nature reserve with discovery tours. There are now even property agents and PR activities. The main areas are Cahuita and Puerto Viejo on the Caribbean coast, Playa Sámara in the north and Golfito in the south. And the northern Pacific coast is the new home for North American retirees.

600 m/1,968 ft. Wear appropriate clothing, insect repellents and a mosquito net to protect yourself.

The water companies warn against the drinking water outside San José. So avoid ice cubes and opt for mineral water.

HOSTELS

For a list of youth hostels and similar accommodation (with a booking option), go to *www.hostelworld.com/hostels/Costa-Rica*. Prices vary between US$10 and 20 for a night. A list of youth hostels is available in San José from the *Albergue Juvenil Toruma (Av. Central/C/ 29–31 | tel. 22 34 81 86 | www.hosteltoruma.com)*.

HOTELS

Hotel prices vary greatly between the seasons, dropping by almost half between May and October, in the rainy season ("green season"). In recent years in particular, international 4- and 5-star hotels have opened in various towns in the highlands that appeal to tourists, as well as on popular beaches. All in all, the country continues to attract people who prefer rustic lodges and small individually operated guesthouses. The seal **INSIDER TIP** *Tucan Hotels (www.tucan-hotels.com)* is a group of eleven small, well-prices establishments that can be found all over the country.

IMMIGRATION

British citizens do not need a visa and may stay as a visitors in Costa Rica for up to 90 days under a tourist visa waiver. Your passport should have at least one day's validity from the date you are leaving Costa Rica.

US-Americans do not require an entry visa to Costa Rica, but need a current

CURRENCY CONVERTER

£	CRC	CRC	£
1	757.27	1,000	1.32
2	1,514.54	2,000	2.64
3	2,271.81	2,500	3.30
4	3,029.08	3,000	3.96
5	3,786.35	4,000	5.28
6	4,543.62	5,000	6.60
7	5,300.89	7,000	9.24
8	6,058.16	8,000	10.56
9	6,815.43	9,000	11.88

US$	CRC	CRC	US$
1	596.86	1,000	1.68
2	1,193.72	2,000	3.36
3	1,790.58	2,500	4.20
4	2,387.44	3,000	5.04
5	2,984.30	4,000	6.72
6	3,581.16	5,000	8.40
7	4,178.02	7,000	11.76
8	4,774.88	8,000	13.44
9	5,371.74	9,000	15.12

For current exchange rates see www.xe.com

valid passport and a return ticket to exit Costa Rica within 90 days.

INFORMATION

Costa Rica does not have an information office in Europe. Tourist information is available from the *Embassy of Costa Rica (14 Lancaster Gate) London W2 3LH | tel. 020 7706 8844 | www.costarica.embassy homepage.com)*. The official Costa Rican tourism institutions ICT (Instituto Costarricense de Turismo) and Canatur (Cámara Nacional de Turismo) have only a few information offices in Costa Rica. In many cases, travel agencies and tour operators have assumed this function. The *Centre of the ICT (Autopista General Cañas 1 | East side of Juan Pablo II Bridge, Uruca | tel. 22 99 58 00)* resides in San José.

There is plenty of information on the ICT website, www.visitcostarica.com, including in English.

NATIONAL PARKS

Humidity and temperatures are high in the national parks and protected areas. You'll need multi-functional clothing and comfortable hiking boots. Take water and perhaps a snack, as these can usually only be purchased at the entrances to the parks and protected areas. You should always expect rain, so it's a good idea to take a lightweight rainproof jacket with you. At the Corcovado and Tortuguero Parks *guides* are compulsory, otherwise you can decide for yourself whether to explore the wilderness alone with a map or would rather have animals and special plants pointed out to you. Most of the parks are open between 7am and 3pm. Admission to the state parks is around US$15.

PERSONAL SAFETY

Costa Rico is a very safe country to visit. A higher crime level really only affects the capital San José, Puerto Limón and Moín on the Caribbean coast, where there are increasing armed robberies in the evenings and in dark areas. Poverty and unemployment, petty crime and car burglaries are also increasing as the result of cost-cutting and massive tax increases introduced at the end of 2018.

Follow these tips to travel safely: do not travel on public buses after dark, and especially at night. Always take someone with you to an ATM. When going out for the day, only take as much money with you as you will need for the day; leave the rest in the hotel safe. Never leave valuables or large items of luggage in a hire car.

PHONE & MOBILE PHONE

The international dial code for Costa Rica is *00506,* from Costa Rica to the UK it is *0044,* to the United States *001*

Prepaid SIM cards for tourists are available from 3,000 colones, and obtainable from the ICE desk in the Arrivals hall of the airport and at ICE points. The Costa Rican network providers Claro CR *(www. claro.cr)* and Movistar *(www.movistar.cr)* offer SIM cards ("chip") with rates from 6 cents/minute to the Costa Rican landline system, and from 8 cents/minute to mobile phones.

POST

At the time of going to print, the rate for an airmail letter or postcard to Europe is 665 colones.

PUBLIC TRANSPORT

Buses connect the capital San José to all the towns and every part of the country. They are extremely reasonable, but often packed, especially at the weekends. The private companies have their own stations (more than ten in San José), and a bus timetable (available from the ICT and hotels) provides information on their locations and destinations. For long-distance destinations and weekend travel, it's best to purchase your tickets in advance. The private company **INSIDER TIP** *Quality Transfers (www.qualitytransferscr. com)* operates six- to 12-seater minibuses to all the tourist destinations daily, including from hotel to hotel.

There are also lots of ferries around the Gulf of Nicoya and across the estuary of the Río Tempisque. There is an important connection in the south from Golfito to Puerto Jiménez and a ferry to Rincón.

TAXI

Taxi rides can be annoying in Costa Rica, especially in San José. If the taximeter *(maría)* is on, then journeys are very cheap, but this is rare. Drivers don't switch it on, or fail to reset it so that the previous amount is included in your fare. The *maría* might have been manipulated (you'll hear a loud clicking) or the driver tells you it's broken. Threatening to call a traffic policeman *(tránsito)* rarely makes any difference. The 50+ rule often helps: older drivers are usually more honest.

TIME

GMT minus 6 hours, and minus 7 hours during European summer time.

TIPPING

Service is included in the bill in restaurants, and although the Costa Ricans don't usually tip it is expected of tourists. Guide for tipping in hotels: chambermaids receive about 300 colones per night, porters 200 per item.

WI-FI

Meanwhile WLAN *(wifi)* is available in most hotels and guesthouses. It is also possible to log on free using a password in many cafés and restaurants, although access may occasionally be unavailable, especially in remote regions and during the rainy season.

WOMEN TRAVELLING SOLO

In "macho" Costa Rica, women travelling alone will receive not only curious looks, but other "attention" as well. However, there is no particular danger, although by the same token they should not be out and about in San José and Puerto Limón after dark nor on isolated beaches.

WEATHER IN SAN JOSÉ

	Jan.	Feb.	March	April	May	June	July	Aug.	Sept.	Oct.	Nov.	Dec.
Daytime temperature in °C/°F	24/75	24/75	26/79	27/81	27/81	27/81	26/79	26/79	27/81	26/79	25/77	24/75
Night-time temperatures in °C/°F	14/57	14/57	15/59	16/61	16/61	16/61	16/61	16/61	16/61	15/59	15/59	15/59
Sunshine hours/day	7	8	8	7	5	4	4	4	5	4	4	6
Precipitation days/month	1	0	1	4	17	20	18	19	20	22	14	4

USEFUL PHRASES SPANISH

PRONUNCIATION

c	before 'e' and 'i' like 'th' in 'thin'
ch	as in English
g	before 'e' and 'i' like the 'ch' in Scottish 'loch'
gue, gui	like 'get', 'give'
que, qui	the 'u' is not spoken, i.e. 'ke', 'ki'
j	always like the 'ch' in Scottish 'loch'
ll	like 'lli' in 'million'; some speak it like 'y' in 'yet'
ñ	'nj'
z	like 'th' in 'thin'

IN BRIEF

Yes/No/Maybe	sí/no/quizás
Please/Thank you	por favor/gracias
Hello!/Goodbye!/See you	¡Hola!/¡Adiós!/¡Hasta luego!
Good morning!/afternoon!/evening!/night!	¡Buenos días!/¡Buenos días!/¡Buenas tardes!/¡Buenas noches!
Excuse me, please!	¡Perdona!/¡Perdone!
May I...?/Pardon?	¿Puedo...?/¿Cómo dice?
My name is...	Me llamo...
What's your name?	¿Cómo se llama usted?/¿Cómo te llamas?
I'm from...	Soy de...
I would like to.../Have you got...?	Querría.../¿Tiene usted...?
How much is...?	¿Cuánto cuesta...?
I (don't) like that	Esto (no) me gusta.
good/bad/broken/doesn't work	bien/mal/roto/no funciona
too much/much/little/all/nothing	demasiado/mucho/poco/todo/nada
Help!/Attention!/Caution!	¡Socorro!/¡Atención!/¡Cuidado!
ambulance/police/fire brigade	ambulancia/policía/bomberos
May I take a photo here	¿Podría fotografiar aquí?

DATE & TIME

Monday/Tuesday/Wednesday	lunes/martes/miércoles
Thursday/Friday/Saturday	jueves/viernes/sábado
Sunday/working day/holiday	domingo/laborable/festivo
today/tomorrow/yesterday	hoy/mañana/ayer
hour/minute/second/moment	hora/minuto/segundo/momento

¿Hablas español?

'Do you speak Spanish?' This guide will help you
to say the basic words and phrases in Spanish.

day/night/week/month/year	día/noche/semana/mes/año
now/immediately/before/after	ahora/enseguida/antes/despúes
What time is it?	¿Qué hora es?
It's three o'clock/It's half past three	Son las tres/Son las tres y media
a quarter to four/a quarter past four	cuatro menos cuarto/ cuatro y cuarto

TRAVEL

open/closed/opening times	abierto/cerrado/horario
entrance/exit	entrada/acceso salida
departure/arrival	salida/llegada
toilets/ladies/gentlemen	aseos/señoras/caballeros
free/occupied	libre/ocupado
(not) drinking water	agua (no) potable
Where is...?/Where are...?	¿Dónde está...? /¿Dónde están...?
left/right	izquierda/derecha
straight ahead/back	recto/atrás
close/far	cerca/lejos
traffic lights/corner/crossing	semáforo/esquina/cruce
bus/tram/U-underground/	autobús/tranvía/metro/
taxi/cab	taxi
bus stop/cab stand	parada/parada de taxis
parking lot/parking garage	parking/garaje
street map/map	plano de la ciudad/mapa
train station/harbour/airport	estación/puerto/aeropuerto
ferry/quay	transbordador/muelle
schedule/ticket/supplement	horario/billete/suplemento
single/return	sencillo/ida y vuelta
train/track/platform	tren/vía/andén
delay/strike	retraso/huelga
I would like to rent...	Querría... alquilar
a car/a bicycle/a boat	un coche/una bicicleta/un barco
petrol/gas station	gasolinera
petrol/gas/diesel	gasolina/diesel
breakdown/repair shop	avería/taller

FOOD & DRINK

Could you please book a table for tonight for four?	Resérvenos, por favor, una mesa para cuatro personas para hoy por la noche.
on the terrace/by the window	en la terraza/junto a la ventana
The menu, please!	¡El menú, por favor!

Could I please have...?	¿Podría traerme... por favor?
bottle/carafe/glass	botella/jarra/vaso
knife/fork/spoon	cuchillo/tenedor/cuchara
salt/pepper/sugar	sal/pimienta/azúcar
vinegar/oil/milk/cream/lemon	vinagre/aceite/leche/limón
cold/too salty/not cooked	frío/demasiado salado/sin hacer
with/without ice/sparkling	con/sin hielo/gas
vegetarian/allergy	vegetariano/vegetariana/alergía
May I have the bill, please?	Querría pagar, por favor.
bill/receipt/tip	cuenta/recibo/propina

SHOPPING

pharmacy/chemist	farmacia/droguería
baker/market	panadería/mercado
butcher/fishmonger	carnicería/pescadería
shopping centre/department store	centro comercial/grandes almacenes
shop/supermarket/kiosk	tienda/supermercado/quiosco
100 grammes/1 kilo	cien gramos/un kilo
expensive/cheap/price/more/less	caro/barato/precio/más/menos
organically grown	de cultivo ecológico

ACCOMMODATION

I have booked a room	He reservado una habitación.
Do you have any... left?	¿Tiene todavía...?
single room/double room	habitación individual/habitación doble
breakfast/half board/	desayuno/media pensión/
full board (American plan)	pensión completa
at the front/seafront/garden view	hacia delante/hacia el mar/hacia el jardín
shower/sit-down bath	ducha/baño
balcony/terrace	balcón/terraza
key/room card	llave/tarjeta
luggage/suitcase/bag	equipaje/maleta/bolso
swimming pool/spa/sauna	piscina/spa/sauna
soap/toilet paper/nappy (diaper)	jabón/papel higiénico/pañal
cot/high chair/nappy changing	cuna/trona/cambiar los pañales
deposit	anticipo/caución

BANKS, MONEY & CREDIT CARDS

bank/ATM/	banco/cajero automático/
pin code	número secreto
cash/credit card	en efectivo/tarjeta de crédito
bill/coin/change	billete/moneda/cambio

HEALTH

doctor/dentist/paediatrician	médico/dentista/pediatra
hospital/emergency clinic	hospital/urgencias
fever/pain/inflamed/injured	fiebre/dolor/inflamado/herido
diarrhoea/nausea/sunburn	diarrea/náusea/quemadura de sol
plaster/bandage/ointment/cream	tirita/vendaje/pomada/crema
pain reliever/tablet/suppository	calmante/comprimido/supositorio

POST, TELECOMMUNICATIONS & MEDIA

stamp/letter/postcard	sello/carta/postal
I need a landline phone card/	Necesito una tarjeta telefónica/
I'm looking for a prepaid card for my mobile	Busco una tarjeta prepago para mi móvil
Where can I find internet access?	¿Dónde encuentro un acceso a internet?
dial/connection/engaged	marcar/conexión/ocupado
socket/adapter/charger	enchufe/adaptador/cargador
computer/battery/ rechargeable battery	ordenador/batería/ batería recargable
e-mail address/at sign (@)	(dirección de) correo electrónico/arroba
internet address (URL)	dirección de internet
internet connection/wifi	conexión a internet/wifi
e-mail/file/print	archivo/imprimir

LEISURE, SPORTS & BEACH

beach/sunshade/lounger	playa/sombrilla/tumbona
low tide/high tide/current	marea baja/marea alta/corriente

NUMBERS

0	cero	14	catorce
1	un, uno, una	15	quince
2	dos	16	dieciséis
3	tres	17	diecisiete
4	cuatro	18	dieciocho
5	cinco	19	diecinueve
6	seis	20	veinte
7	siete	100	cien, ciento
8	ocho	200	doscientos, doscientas
9	nueve	1,000	mil
10	diez	2,000	dos mil
11	once	10,000	diez mil
12	doce	1/2	medio
13	trece	1/4	un cuarto

ROAD ATLAS

The green line indicates the Discovery Tour "Costa Rica at a glance"
The blue line indicates the other Discovery Tours

All tours are also marked on the pull-out map

Photo: Beach at Manuel Antonio National Park

Exploring Costa Rica

The map on the back cover shows how
the area has been sub-divided

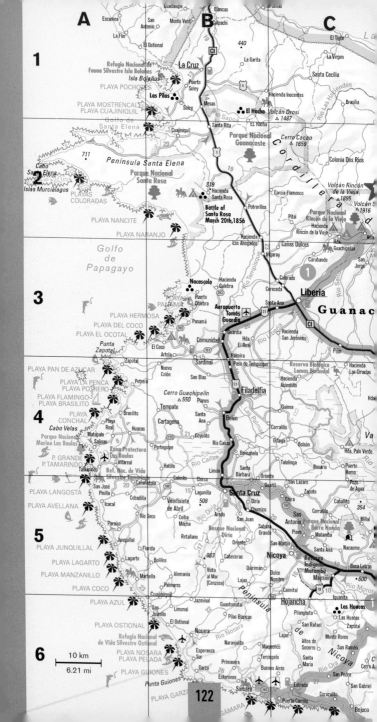

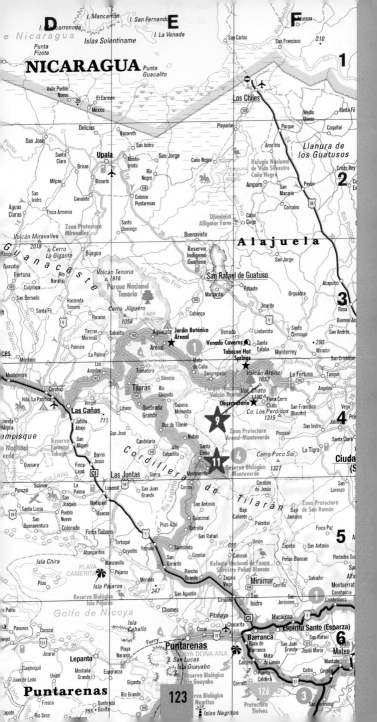

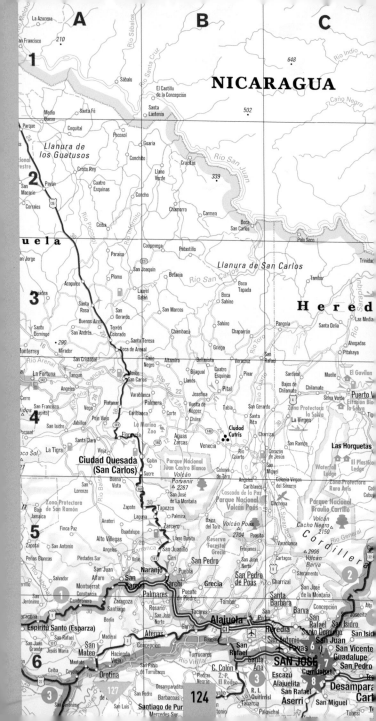

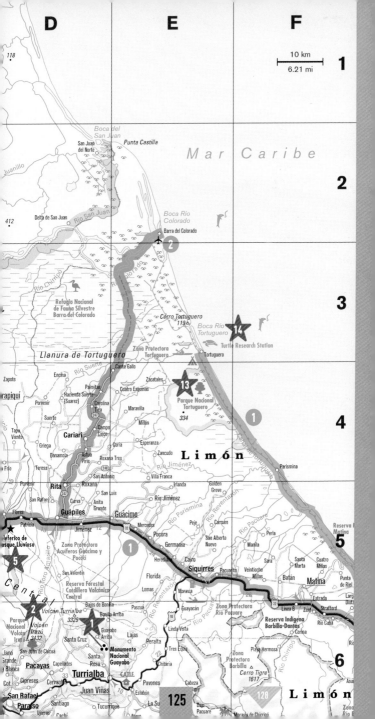

10 km
6.21 mi

1

2

3

4

5

6

Mar Caribe

Boca del
San Juan   Punta Castilla

San Juan
del Norte

118

Juanillo

Delta de San Juan   Río San Juan

412

Boca Río
Colorado

Barra del Colorado ⊗ 2

Río Colorado

Refugio Nacional
de Fauna Silvestre
Barra del Colorado

Río Chirripó

Cerro Tortuguero
119 △

Boca Río
Tortuguero ★ 14
Turtle Research Station

Llanura de Tortuguero

Zona Protectora
Tortuguero

Río Suerte   Canta Gallo   Tortuguero

Zapote

Encina   Palmitas   Zácatales

Hacienda Suerte
(Suárez)   Cuatro Esquinas

★ 13
Parque Nacional
Tortuguero
334

rapiqui

Porvenir   Carolina
Tica   Maravilla

Suerte   247   Campo
Cinco   Milton

Tapa
Viento   **Cariari**   Esperanza

Curia

Griega   Astua
Pirie   Zancudo

Banamola   Roxana Tres

Frio   San Antonio   Villa Franca   Irlanda

Teresa   801

Porvenir   Roxana   **L i m ó n**

Rita   Curva   San Luis   Río Jiménez

San Rafael   247   Anita
Grande   Golden
Grove

Flores   **Guápiles**   **Guácimo**

Río Jiménez

Parismina

Río Toro Amarillo

Patricia   Jiménez   32   Mercedes

eleférico de
osque Lluvioso ★ 5

Zona Protectora
Acuíferos Guácimo y
Pococí

Pocora   Peje   Carmen

Germania   San Alberto
Nuevo

Río Parismina

Perla

Reserva
Matina

Río Pacuare

1

C e n t r a l

San Valentín   Heredian   Cairo

Reserva Forestal
Cordillera Volcánica
Central   Florida   **Siquirres**

Pacuarito   Veintiocho
Millas

Santa
Marta   Cuatro
Millas

Río Reventazón

Lomas   Moravia

Batán   Punta
de Riel

★ 2
Parque
Nacional
Volcán
Irazú △ 3432   Volcán Turrialba
3329

Bajas de Bonilla   Bonilla Arriba

Guayacán

Zona Protectora
Río Pacuare

Matina

Estrada   Larg
Dist

Línea B   Zent

Strafford

llano
Grande
i Blanca   **Pacayas**

△ 1

San Juan de Chicuá

Capellades

Santa
Cruz   Guayabo
Arriba

Lajas   Linda Vista

Reserva Indígena
Barbilla-Dantas

Corona

Río Cuba

Ri

Cot   Cipreses

Volcán
Irazú △ 3432

**Monumento
Nacional
Guayabo**

Peralta   Tres Equis

Zona
Protectora
Barbilla

Playa Hermosa

Cervant

Santa
Rosa

Chitaria

Cerro Tigre
1617 △

Río Chirripó

L i m ó n

**San Rafael
Paraíso**   Santiago

Juan Viñas   10

Turrialba   CATIE

Pavones   Cabeza

Ujarrás   Tucurrique   Eslabón

Cachí   La Su

125

128 ▽

Baja
Pacuare

Morav de Chirripó

Asu

Zona

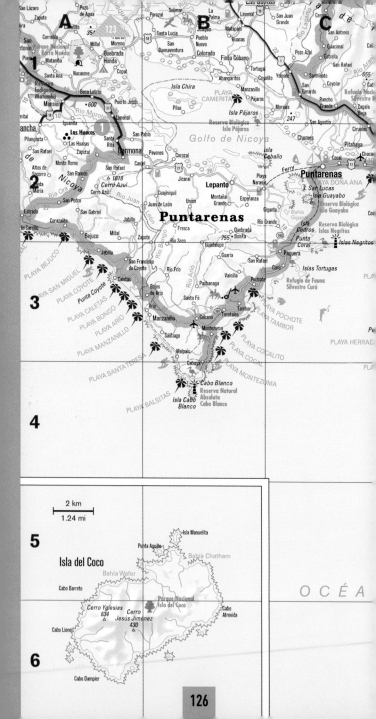

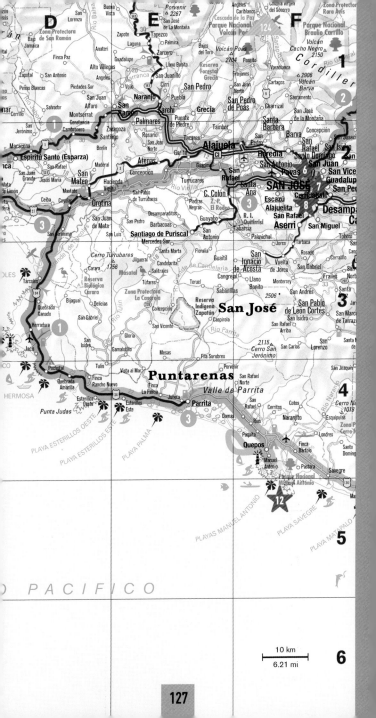

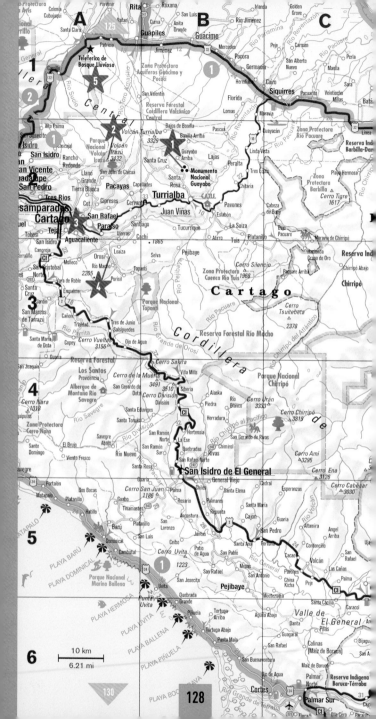

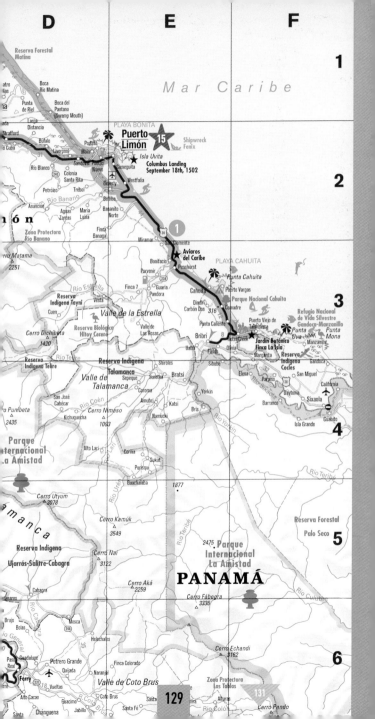

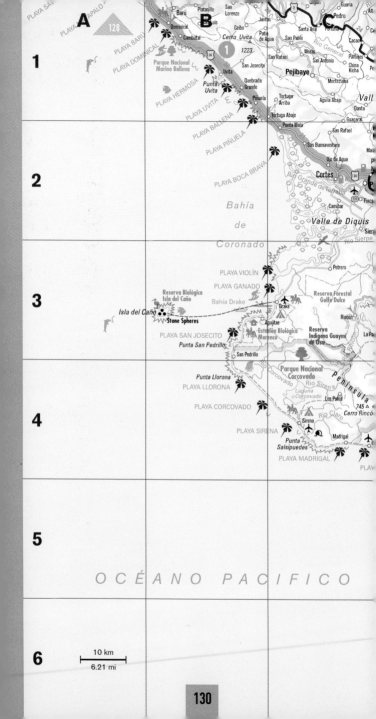

PLAYA SANDIAPALO

A

128

PLAYA BARÚ
PLAYA DOMINICAL

Barú
Dominical
Cambutal
Parque Nacional
Marino Ballena
Punta
Uvita
PLAYA HERMOSA
PLAYA UVITA
PLAYA BALLENA
PLAYA PIÑUELA
PLAYA BOCA BRAVA

B

Platanillo
San Lorenzo
Luis
Ceibo
Cerro Uvita
1223
Uvita
Quebrada
Grande
Piñuela
Tortuga
Arriba
Tortuga Abajo
Punta Mala
San Buenaventura
Ojo de Agua
San Josecito
Patio
de Agua
San Pablo
San Rafael
Masa
San Antonio
San Josecito
Pejibaye
Moctezuma
Aguila Abajo
San Rafael

C

Guaria
Alt
San Pedro
Santa Ana
Cacaon
Río General
Pavones
China
Kisha
Pr
Vall
Danta
Guagaral

Río Grande de Térraba
Cortes
34
Cambar
Finca
Valle de Diquis
Sier

Bahía
de
Coronado

Río Sierpe

PLAYA VIOLÍN
PLAYA GANADO
Bahía Drake
Drake
Aguajitas
Estación Biológica
Marenco
Punta San Pedrillo
San Pedrillo

Reserva Biológica
Isla del Caño
Isla del Caño
Stone Spheres
PLAYA SAN JOSECITO

Reserva Forestal
Golfo Dulce
Rincón
Reserva
Indígena Guaymí
de Osa
La Pa

3

Potrero

Punta Llorona
PLAYA LLORONA
PLAYA CORCOVADO
PLAYA SIRENA
Punta
Salsipuedes
PLAYA MADRIGAL

Parque Nacional
Corcovado
Río Corcovado
Laguna
Corcovado
Sirena
Los Patos
Río Siren
Río Claro
Madrigal
Cerro Rincón
745

Península

PLAY

4

5

OCÉANO   PACÍFICO

6

10 km
6.21 mi

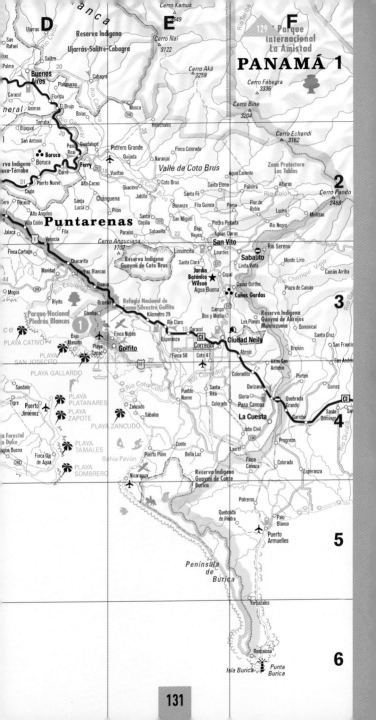

MAP LEGEND

Expressway
Autobahn
Autostrada
Autopista

Highway
Fernverkehrsstraße
Strada di transito
Autovía

Important main road
Wichtige Hauptstraße
Strada di interesse regionale
Carretera general importante

Main road
Hauptstraße
Strada principale
Carretera principal

Secondary road
Nebenstraße
Strada secondaria
Carretera secundaria

Roadway • Pavement
Fahrweg • Fußweg
Strada carrozzabile • Sentiero
Calzada • Sendero

Pan-American Highway
Panamericana
Strada Grande Panamericana
Carretera Interamericana

Distance in km • Checkpoint
Entfernung in km • Grenzübergang
Distanza in km • Stazione di controllo
Distancia en kms • Puesto de control

Road numbering: national • regional
Straßennummerierung: national • regional
Numerazione stradale: nazionale • regionale
Numeración de carreteras: nacional • regional

Railway
Eisenbahn
Ferrovia
Ferrocarril

State boundary • Province boundary
Landesgrenze • Provinzgrenze
Confine di stato • Confine di provincia
Frontera de estado • Límite provincial

Indigenous reserve
Indianerreservat
Riserva indiana
Reserva indígena

Mangrove • Yolillal palms
Mangroven • Yolillalpalmen
Mangrovia • Palma di yolillal
Manglar • Yolillal

Reef • Rocks
Riff • Felsen
Banco • Roccia
Arrecife • Rocas

Dam • Cascade
Staudamm • Wasserfall
Argine • Cascata
Muro de presa • Cascada

Int. Airport • Airfield
Int. Flughafen • Flugplatz
Aeroporto int. • Aerodromo
Aeropuerto int. • Aeródromo

Lighthouse • Golf
Leuchtturm • Golf
Faro • Golf
Faro • Golf

Point of interest • Archaeological site
Sehenswürdigkeit • Archäologische Stätte
Curiosità • Luogo archeologico
Curiosidad • Lugar arqueológico

Cave (submarine) • Petrol station
Höhle (unterseeisch) • Tankstelle
Grotta (sottomarina) • Stazione di rifornimento
Cueva (submarina) • Estación de servicio

Youth hostel • Water-skiing
Jugendherberge • Wasserski
Albergo per la gioventù • Sci nautico
Albergue juvenil • Esquí acuático

Int. Harbour • Yachting
Int. Hafen • Yachthafen
Porto int. • Marina
Puerto int. • Marina

Kayaking • Motor boat
Kajak • Motorboot
Kayak • Barca a motore
Káyac • Lancha de motor

Surfing • Windsurfing
Wellenreiten • Windsurfen
Aquaplane • Surfing
Surf • Windsurf

Deep sea fishing • Scuba diving
Hochseefischen • Sporttauchen
Pesca d'alto mare • Sport subacqueo
Pesca de altura • Submarinismo

Turtle protection area
Schutzzone für Meeresschildkröten
Protettorato di tartarughe marine
Zona de protección de tortugas marinas

National park (marine)
Nationalpark (marin)
Parco nazionale (marino)
Parque nacional (marino)

Nature preserve
Naturreservat
Riserva naturale
Reserva natural

Birdwatching
Vogelbeobachtung
Osservazione di uccelli
Observación de aves

Biological station/Lodge
Biologische Forschungsstation/Hütte
Stazione di ricerca biologica/Capanna
Estación biológica/Cabaña

Riding
Reiten
Equitazione
Paseos a caballo

Camping site • Beach
Campingplatz • Strand
Campeggio • Spiaggia
Camping • Playa

Capital city
Hauptstadt
Capitale di stato
Capital de estado

SAN JOSÉ

Province capital
Provinzhauptstadt
Capoluogo di provincia
Capital de provincia

Heredia

Canton capital
Kantonshauptstadt
Capoluogo di cantone
Capital de cantón

Paraíso

MARCO POLO Discovery Tour 1
MARCO POLO Erlebnistour 1
MARCO POLO Giro awentura 1
MARCO POLO Recorrido aventura 1

MARCO POLO Highlight

MARCO POLO Discovery Tours
MARCO POLO Erlebnistouren
MARCO POLO Giri awenturosi
MARCO POLO Recorridos de aventura

MARCO POLO TRAVEL GUIDES

INDEX

This index lists all places, beaches, national parks, animal reserves and other destinations (e. g. volcanoes) mentioned in this guide. Page numbers in bold type refer to the main entry.

WRITE TO US

e-mail: info@marcopologuides.co.uk

Did you have a great holiday?
Is there something on your mind?
Whatever it is, let us know!
Whether you want to praise, alert us
to errors or give us a personal tip –
MARCO POLO would be pleased to
hear from you.
We do everything we can to provide the
very latest information for your trip.

Nevertheless, despite all of our authors'
thorough research, errors can creep in.
MARCO POLO does not accept any
liability for this. Please contact us by
e-mail or post.
MARCO POLO Travel Publishing Ltd
Pinewood, Chineham Business Park
Crockford Lane, Chineham
Basingstoke, Hampshire RG24 8AL
United Kingdom

PICTURE CREDITS
Cover photograph: Beach at Manuel Antonio (Look: F. M. Frei)
Photos: awlimages: J. Coletti (20/21, 25, 49, 61), F. R. Iacomino (100/101), N. Ledger (52), N. Pavitt (86), F. Ricardo Iacomino (85), A. Robinson (55); awlimages/John Warburton-Lee Photography Ltd.: N. Pavitt (2); Casas Pelicano: Jochen Sperling (19 top); Kathy Dyhr (19 bottom); Four Seasons Resorts Costa Rica at Peninsula Papagaya: Robb Gordon (18 top); Getty Images/Flickr/Pangea Photography: Andrew Burson (5); huber-images: P. Canali (30, 64/65, 88/89, 96, 120/121), P. Giocoso (22), Schmid (flap right), R. Taylor (10, 34, 75); © iStockphoto: Phil Berry (18 bottom); © iStockphoto/nicolebranan (18 centre); Laif: Gonzalez (42, 47, 77, 108 top), T. Hauser (4 bottom, 6, 80), A. Schumacher (99); Laif/hemis.fr: B. Gardel (flap left); Look: F. M. Frei (1 top); mauritius images/age fotostock: T. Montford (70), J. C. Muñoz (69); mauritius images/Alamy (3, 8, 11, 28 right, 29, 102, 107), T. Cohen (66, 106), J. Csernoch (95), M. Dwyer (106/107), R. Granieri (50/51), C. Wise (62); mauritius images/Alamy/robertharding (37); mauritius images/Danita Delimont: C. Miller Hopkins (44); mauritius images/Imagebroker: Siepmann (82); mauritius images/John Warburton-Lee: M. Simoni (32/33); mauritius images/Radius Images (26/27); mauritius images/robertharding (56/57, M. Simoni (40); mauritius images/Universal Images Group (104); mauritius images/Westend61: S. Roesch (28 left); H. Mielke (4 top, 17, 30/31, 31, 39, 58, 78/79, 105, 108 bottom, 109); Schapowalow: G. Cozzi (7), R. Schmid (12/13, 72); Schapowalow/SIME: P. Canali (9, 14/15); M. Zegers (104/105)

1st edition 2020
Worldwide Distribution: Marco Polo Travel Publishing Ltd, Pinewood, Chineham
Business Park, Crockford Lane, Basingstoke, Hampshire RG24 8AL, United Kingdom. Email: sales@marcopolouk.com
© MAIRDUMONT GmbH & Co. KG, Ostfildern
Author: Birgit Müller-Wöbcke; editor: Petra Klose
What's hot: wunder media, Munich, Birgit Müller-Wöbcke
Cartography road atlas: © Berndtson & Berndtson Productions GmbH, Fürstenfeldbruck; cartography pull-out map: © Berndtson & Berndtson Productions GmbH, Fürstenfeldbruck
Cover design, p. 1, pull-out map cover: Karl Anders – Studio für Brand Profiling, Hamburg; design inside: milchhof:atelier, Berlin; design p. 2/3, Discovery Tours: Susan Chaaban Dipl.-Des. (FH)
Translated from German by Mo Croasdale
Editorial office: SAW Communications, Redaktionsbüro Dr. Sabine A. Werner, Mainz: Julia Gilcher, Cosima Talhouni, Dr. Sabine A. Werner; prepress: SAW Communications, Mainz, in cooperation with alles mit Medien, Mainz

MIX
Paper from
responsible sources
FSC® C124385

DOS AND DON'TS 👆

There are some things you should not do in Costa Rica

BE CARELESS

Compared with other Latin American countries, Costa Rica is almost a paradise. But there is a layer of very poor people, which includes about 200,000 refugees from Nicaragua, who have no income. It's better not to carry a lot with you if you are walking around San José, Puntarenas or Limón, and do not wear any jewellery. And when visiting a restaurant, sit by the window or outside so you can always see your fully-laden hire car!

GET MIXED UP IN DRUGS

There are numerous offers on the Caribbean coast, but the police doesn't see the funny side even if "soft" drugs are involved. For a long time, Costa Rica was considered a trading centre for drug dealing between South America and the USA, and the country is now trying hard to put paid to this reputation. So practise saying a firm *no, gracias*.

UNDERESTIMATE THE CURRENT

Careful when swimming: there are dangerous currents all along the Pacific coast and on the southern Atlantic – sometimes even when the water only goes up to your knees. Never swim in the open sea, but keep to the bays. Never let small children out of your sight. There are not many lifeguards on the beach, so better do what the locals do.

BUY SOUVENIRS WITHOUT THINKING

Among the many souvenirs on offer are some that are of concern to animal protection organisations: bags made of crocodile and snake skin, animal pelts, items made of tortoiseshell, tortoise shells, rare shells and corals, and jewellery made from them. Importing these items to your home country is forbidden anyway.

SMOKE IN THE WRONG PLACE

Costa Rica has strict non-smoking laws. Smoking is legally forbidden in all public facilities, hotels (on the entire premises), restaurants (even open-air ones), bars, buses, markets, in parks and on beaches. Failure to observe the law could cost you up to US$800!

ORDER SHARK FINS

The trade in shark fins is forbidden in Costa Rica, but it is widespread along the Pacific coast. Taiwanese fishing companies have fishing boats here, and most of the catch goes to Asia. Robbed of their fins, the sharks die a slow and painful death. So please avoid the shark fin soup in restaurants.

DRIVE AT NIGHT

Potholes are common on the roads, and deep holes can be dangerous. As it is more difficult to see them at night, it's best to leave the car at home.